Inside APPC

Michael Hurwicz

ARCHITECTURE
TECHNOLOGY
CORPORATION
SPECIALISTS IN COMPUTER ARCHITECTURE

P.O. BOX 24344 • MINNEAPOLIS, MINNESOTA 55424 • (612) 935-2035

Printed in the United States of America.

First Printing March 1987

Architecture Technology Corporation
P.O. Box 24344
Minneapolis, MN 55424

Library of Congress Cataloging-in-Publication Data

Communication networks.

Includes index.
1. Computer networks 2. SNA
I. Hurwicz, Michael

ISBN 0-939405-02-4

Illustrations by Architecture Technology Corporation
and Maxim Hurwicz

Table of Contents

List of Figures

DISCLAIMER

FOREWORD

Since 1981, Architecture Technology Corporation (ATC) has gathered and disseminated information on computer architecture and PC LANs. ATC provides consulting and seminars, and publishes newsletters, handbooks, and reports. *Inside APPC*, by Michael Hurwicz, is the third in a series of books covering specific, timely topics in the field of LANs.

Inside APPC is an in-depth monograph delving into Advanced Program-to-Program Communications (APPC) and related technology issues. This very readable book begins with a conceptual and historical overview of APPC, including its relationship to IBM's Systems Network Architecture (SNA), its benefits for users and vendors, and likely future directions. It discusses the APPC architecture, formats and protocols, and compatible products and programs. Finally, it provides detailed examples of how APPC verbs are used.

Because of IBM's importance in the data communications world, and APPC's strategic importance to IBM, *Inside APPC* is essential reading for anyone interested in data communications, particularly in SNA environments.

Architecture Technology Corporation

PREFACE

Advanced Program-to-Program Communications (APPC) is an architecture destined for implementation on an extremely wide range of IBM and non-IBM data communications products. Indeed, the phrase often used in IBM literature in connection with APPC is "any-to-any" connectivity. IBM is presenting APPC as a single solution for corporate distributed processing, covering the gamut of transmission systems, operating systems, hardware, and software. There is no architecture more central to IBM's distributed processing strategy. APPC is clearly important to IBM's customers. Because of IBM's influence in data communications, APPC is also extremely significant for vendors other than IBM, and for users of those vendors' products.

Inside APPC is intended to give the reader an understanding of APPC, both from a practical and from a technical point of view. Based on thousands of pages of IBM source material, it presents general information, analysis, and details of formats and protocols.

I would like to take this opportunity to thank the many people who have helped me during the researching and writing of this book.

Michael Hurwicz
Nashville, Tennessee
February 1987

To My Parents

Chapter 1 - Overview

1.1 The Basic Idea of APPC

"Advanced Program-to-Program Communication" (APPC) is an IBM architecture which enables programs on networked computers to exchange information. IBM bills APPC as a single solution to the communications needs of a diverse group of IBM products, including microcomputers, minicomputers, mainframes, image terminals, and printers. In addition, other major vendors have accepted APPC as the basis for gateways into the IBM world. Thus, APPC offers a software solution to the problem of multivendor connectivity.

By itself, APPC does nothing. A complete APPC configuration requires:

Application programs -- to provide services to end users
Service programs -- which are considered part of APPC and provide services to application programs
APPC -- to support application and service programs
A network -- to provide data link connections for APPC
Computers which support APPC -- to serve as nodes on the network

1.2 Peer-to-Peer versus Terminal-to-Host Communication

APPC is designed for peer-to-peer communication: it allows two programs to communicate as equals. It does not assume a terminal-to-host environment.

Note: APPC and terminal-to-host communications may take place side-by-side. In fact, in the mainframe environment, APPC is built on a base of software designed for terminal-to-host communications. CICS (Customer Information Control System) and an "access method" such as VTAM (Virtual Telecommunications Access Method) are the terminal-to-host communications software which APPC requires in the mainframe environment.

APPC is part of Systems Network Architecture (SNA), which is IBM's master plan for allowing IBM products to communicate with one another. Figure 1-1 shows the logical structure (and, roughly, the historical evolution) of terminal-to-host networks, including SNA networks:

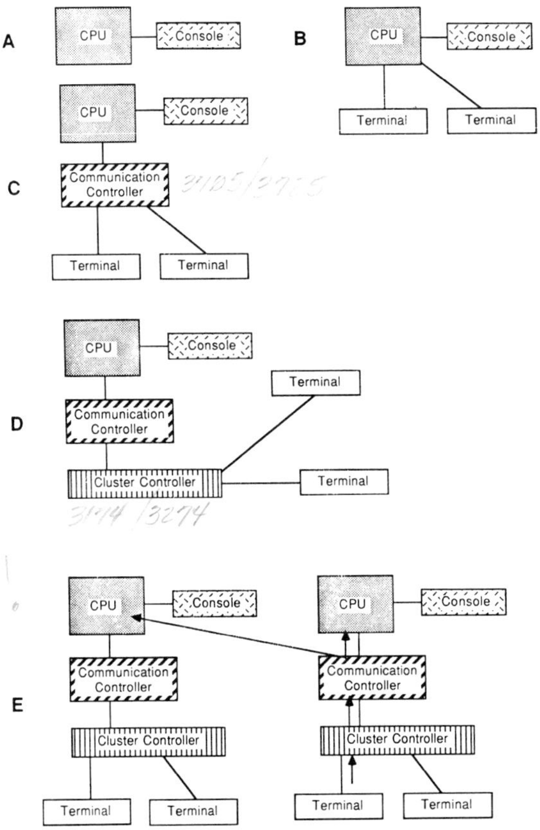

Figure 1-1: Terminal-to-Host Communication

In Figure 1-1, part "a," there is just a central processing unit (CPU) with a console (control operator station).

In order to provide convenient end-user access to the CPU, terminals are added. (Figure 1-1, part "b.")

When communications-related processing begins to overburden the CPU, a communication control unit or "front end" is introduced to handle most of that processing. (Figure 1-1, part "c.")

Next, the cluster controller is inserted, largely in order to save the expense of building into each terminal the logic necessary to use a communications line directly. (Figure 1-1, part "d.")

Finally, one or more communication control units can direct terminal traffic to any one of several CPUs; in Figure 1-1, part "e," all terminals can access either of two hosts through either of two communication control units.

In the terminal-host network in Figure 1-1, there is some intelligence in the communication control unit and the cluster controller, and perhaps even in the terminals. But applications (end-user programs) run only in the CPU. APPC could not be used for the communications shown in Figure 1-1, because: 1) There is no program-to-program (application-to-application) communication. Terminals are the sole sources and destinations for information. Two applications cannot exchange information. 2) There is no peer-to-peer communication. A host has no "equal" on the network with which it can communicate.

Figure 1-2 shows communication between the hosts. APPC could be used for the communication shown in Figure 1-2, because: 1) It could be program-to- program communication. Two applications could exchange information. 2) The two hosts are equals. If they treat each other as such, Figure 1-2 represents peer-to-peer communication.

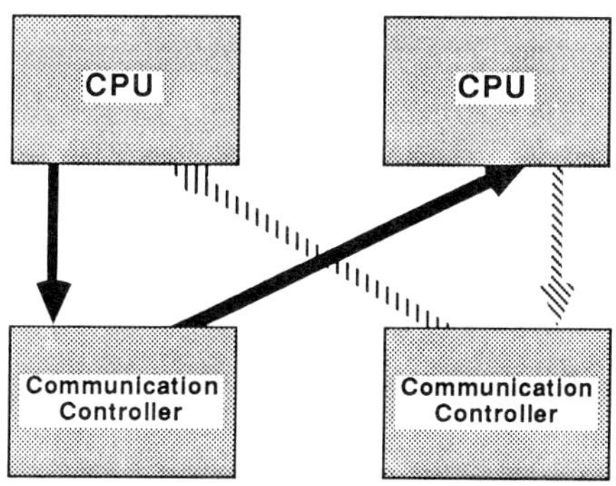

Figure1-2: Host-to-Host Communication

Note that the physical configurations in Figure 1-1 "e" and Figure 1-2 are the same. The information flow, however, is different. There is no CPU-to- CPU information flow in Figure 1-1 "e."

Figure 1-3 shows microcomputers added to the network. If the microcomputers appear as terminals (by running terminal emulation software), then this is just a terminal-host network. Though the PCs are in reality application processors, they don't appear as such to other application processors on the network.

The purpose of APPC is to allow any application processor to appear as such to other application processors on the network. APPC does this by providing program-to-program, peer-to-peer communication between both similar and dissimilar machines.

1.3 SNA and APPC: Data Communication Standards

Introduced in 1974, SNA is now used by about seventy-five percent of the largest corporations in the United States. This percentage appears to be growing, making SNA a well-established de facto data communications standard. IBM reiterates regularly its commitment to SNA as the strategic architecture for its networking products.

Within SNA, APPC is the strategic architecture for program-to-program communication. Since SNA is so deeply-entrenched, APPC holds a secure position in today's data communications environment. Though it is not yet clear how widely APPC will be used by application programmers, it is clear that most major hardware vendors will make the APPC programming interface available on their machines. Because of this wide availability and the unique abilities of APPC, many observers believe it will dominate in those applications for which it is appropriate, such as distributed data processing, file transfer, document distribution, office communications, remote data base access, and network management.

1.4 Historical Limitations of SNA

APPC is based on enhancements to SNA. These enhancements were required because SNA was originally designed as a terminal-to-host communications system. Under this design, there was a basic asymmetry between the terminal and the host, with terminals acting as slaves to host computers. This approach made sense when host computers possessed almost all the intelligence in the network, while terminals possessed very little.

The 1980's, however, saw the rise of the microcomputer, and a dramatic increase in end-user computing power. End-users now began using microcomputers, as well as non-intelligent terminals, to communicate with minicomputers, mainframes, and other microcomputers.

SNA's asymmetrical design imposed two major limitations on the microcomputer in the context of the SNA network. The first limitation had to do with distributed processing, the second with peer-to-peer relationships.

Distributed Processing

Users wanted to distribute processing tasks among microcomputers, minicomputers, and mainframes. Though such distributed processing was not impossible under SNA prior to APPC, neither was there one standard means of implementing it. Furthermore, for distributed processing involving microcomputers, the various non-standard ways which were devised generally required a great deal of rather complex programming, in order to "fool" a host computer into seeing a PC as a non-intelligent device, while still allowing the PC to use its full powers.

Peer-to-Peer Relationships

Users also wanted peer-to-peer relationships among computers, relationships in which control functions could reside in any computer on the network. In a traditional SNA network, the mainframe host controlled the network components in all other nodes. Peripheral nodes, such as workstations, were treated simply as sources and destinations for data.

1.5 IBM's Response

IBM's response to these user needs was two-fold:

First, IBM offered the Token Ring Network as IBM's standard means of high-speed local communication between dissimilar machines. Most types of IBM computers will eventually be able to function as nodes on the ring. The Token Ring is not absolutely necessary for distributed processing or peer- to-peer communications, but it offers advantages over previously available standard local communication methods. Specifically, it is faster than either SDLC (Synchronous Data Link Control) or asynchronous communications, and more reliable than asynchronous communications. Thus, the Token Ring provides an infrastructure which allows faster distributed processing and peer-to-peer communications, without sacrificing reliability. Since most major hardware vendors are likely to support the Token Ring, it will offer these advantages in a multivendor environment, as well.

Second, IBM selected APPC as its central high-level protocol for program-to-program communication. APPC allows peer-to-peer communications and distributed processing between machines using either Token-Ring protocols or SDLC protocols. (There is no theoretical limitation on the types of low- level communications protocols which can be used with APPC. As of late 1986, these two had been used.)

1.6 SNA : Basic Concepts

SNA is a networking architecture which specifies how products connect to and communicate with one another. Products include processors, workstations, and controllers. Each of these may become a "node," or participant, in the SNA network.

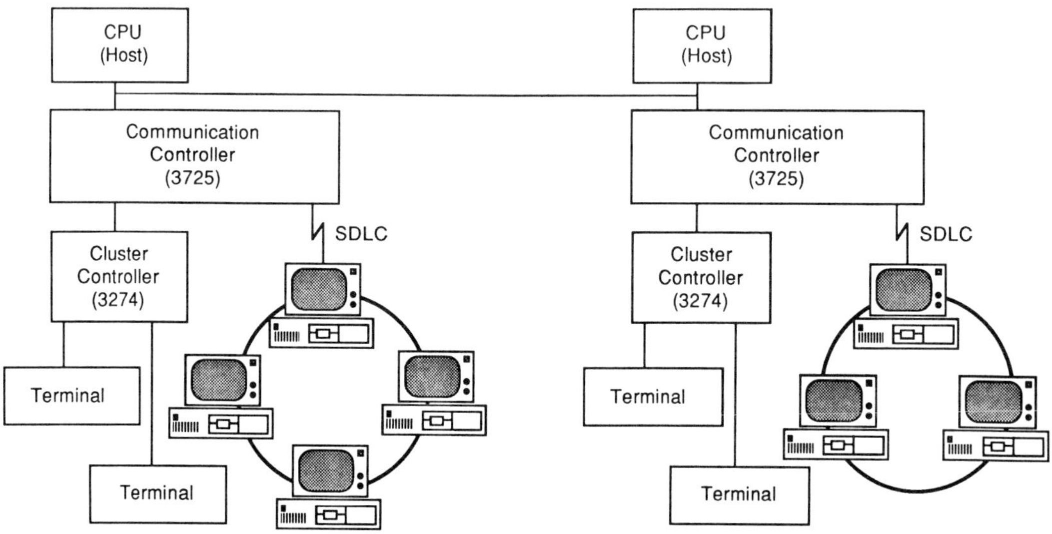

Figure 1-3: SNA Network With PCs

The three most important types of nodes are host nodes, communication controller nodes, and peripheral nodes. In the typical network, the host would be a mainframe, the communication controller would be a 3725 "front end" to the mainframe, and the peripheral node would be a minicomputer, a terminal, or a 3274 Cluster Controller with attached terminals. (See Figure 1-3.)

Within each node, either in software or firmware, are programs implementing SNA functions. One of these programs is the "Logical Unit" (LU). The Logical Unit provides SNA services to end users. End users may be human beings or application programs. An SNA network can be viewed as simply a collection of LUs connected by "sessions" or logical connections. (See Figure 1-4.)

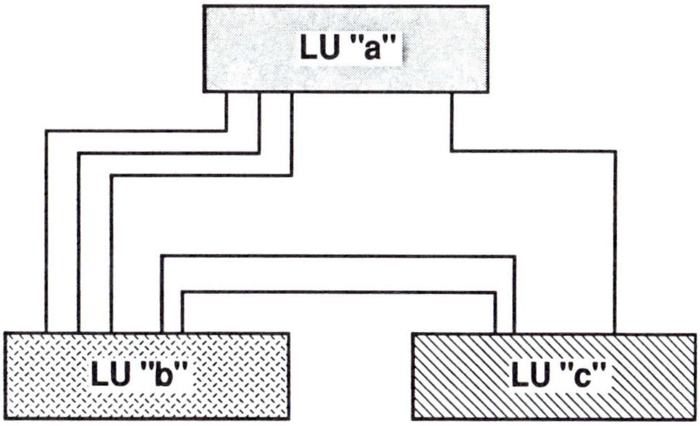

Figure 1-4: LUs Connected By Sessions

Another such program is the Physical Unit, which manages and monitors the node's network resources, such as data links (communication lines).

LUs and PUs come in different varieties, identified by numbers such as LU6.0 and PU2.0.

A PC on an SNA network has in the past often been represented by PU2.0. This means the PC emulated a cluster controller or a batch terminal, implying a master-slave relationship with the host. Furthermore, PCs could not communicate with each other without going through the host (because cluster controllers and terminals are limited in this way).

Programs communicating with other programs on an SNA network have used LU6.0 or LU6.1. These LUs were implemented only in mainframes and minicomputers. To communicate with other products, programs used other LU types, such as type 0, 1, 2 or 3. This was necessary, since each LU can communicate only with another LU of the same type. There was no single LU type which was designed to be used in all products.

1.7 APPC : Basic Concepts

APPC is a particular type of Logical Unit, LU6.2. It is supported by Physical Unit 2.1. LU6.2 allows programs to communicate with other programs. (Human operators do not use APPC directly for communications functions.) Normally, the communicating programs would be on different computers, though a multi-tasking computer can communicate internally using APPC.

Figure 1-5 shows how programs communicate through their respective LUs. The resources available to each program include sessions with other LUs, as well as local files and devices such as printers. Programs can be designed to share resources. Thus, a resource which program "b" uses locally can be used remotely by program "a."

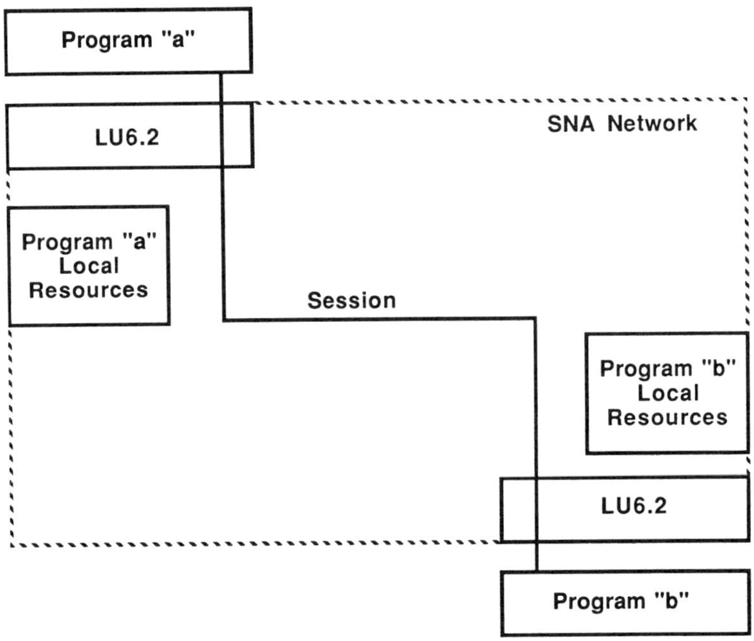

Figure 1-5: Programs Communicating Over A Session

A single instance of a program can communicate with any number of other programs simultaneously. However, APPC thinks in terms of "conversations" which allow program pairs to communicate. Figure 1-6 shows how programs view the communications network.

Figure 1-6: How Programs View The Network

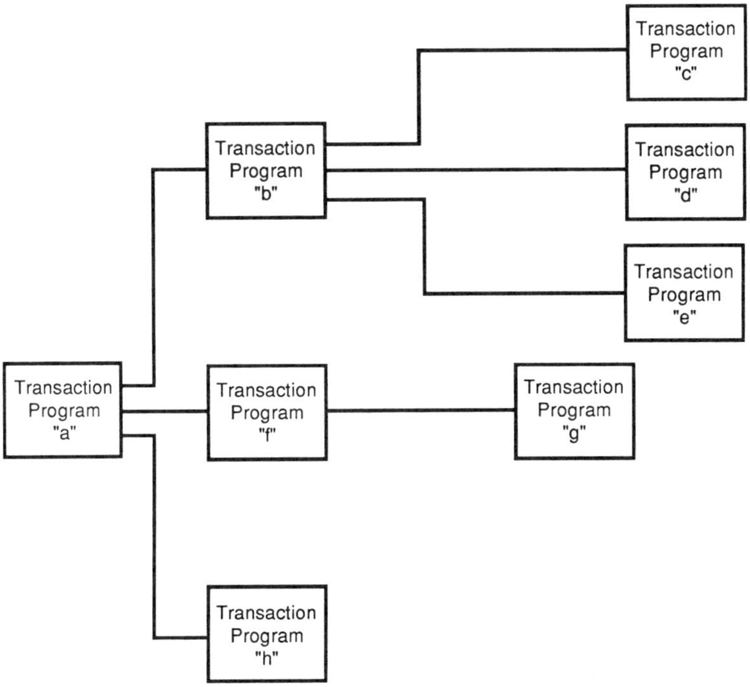

Figure 1-7: One-To-One Conversations

Because of this "one-to-one" viewpoint, APPC does not directly support a broadcast capability. Indirectly, however, broadcasts can be effected. In Figure 1-7, any transaction program can effectively broadcast a message by sending it out over all available conversations and requesting other transaction programs to pass it on. (Transaction programs would have to be written to provide this feature.)

LU6.0 and 6.1, like LU6.2, allow communication between two application programs. LU6.2, however, is enhanced for better support of distributed transaction processing. Similarly, PU2.1 improves upon PU2.0 to offer better support for peer-to-peer connectivity.

Distributed Transaction Processing

A "transaction" is a unit of work performed by an application program. In the past, a transaction was typically associated with a terminal user who requested the transaction, waited for it to complete, requested another transaction, and so on. Transactions can, however, be requested in a similar manner by programs.

A "distributed transaction" is executed cooperatively on multiple systems. A program which performs transactions cooperatively with one or more programs residing on other systems is a "transaction program."

For example, APPC might be used to allow geographically separated stores to order merchandise from one of several warehouses, while recording the transaction and generating bills at a central accounting site. Each ordered item might constitute one transaction, and an APPC-based transaction program would handle the communication between the stores' computers, the computers in the warehouses, and the central accounting computer. (See Figure 1-8.)

Peer-to-Peer Connectivity

The earliest implementations of SNA allowed only terminal-to-host communication. Two terminals could not communicate with one another without going through the host. Later, various forms of peer-to-peer communication were developed. For examples, System/34 minicomputers could use LU6.0 to communicate among themselves directly, while 5520 Administrative Systems could use LU4.0 for the same purpose. LU6.2 is unique in that it is designed to be a standard for peer-to-peer communications, implementable in all systems which perform distributed transaction processing.

In order to implement peer-to-peer connectivity successfully, IBM recognized that a number of capabilities must be permitted to all nodes. In order to create a node

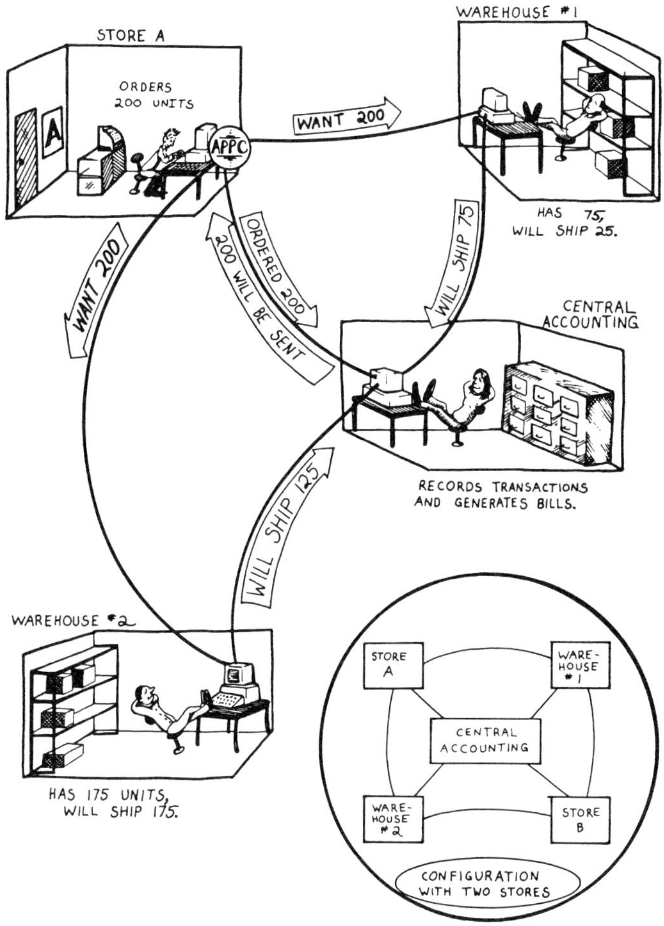

Figure 1-8: Sample APPC Utilization

which would support these functions, IBM chose to enhance PU2.0, creating PU2.1.

The practical result of the new PU2.1 is that a host computer is no longer required to act as an intermediary when two peripheral nodes communicate. The peripheral nodes can communicate directly, on a peer-to-peer basis. (See section 2.7 for more on PU2.1.) Section 3.3 describes how APPN (Application-to-Application Networking) could effect such peer-to-peer connections.

1.8 APPC Benefits

APPC is the first broadly-accepted standard for program-to-program communications. What are the benefits of such a standard? What problems may APPC solve?

Problem: Creating Distributed Transaction Programs

Distributed transaction processing between unlike intelligent systems is often impossible without a standard communication interface designed to support this type of application. This applies to machines within the IBM line, and to machines of different vendors. Though some kind of communication may be possible between the machines, transaction programs are difficult to write when peer-to-peer programming interfaces are different for different machines. Many large organizations have became a patchwork of more or less isolated networks because of this situation.

Figure 1-9 shows two machines connected by low-level communication links. There might be SDLC or Token-Ring links, for example. System B can also emulate a System A terminal. However, none of this permits distributed transaction processing between the two machines. Figure 1-10 shows the addition of a standard application-level peer-to-peer interface such as APPC, permitting distributed transaction processing.

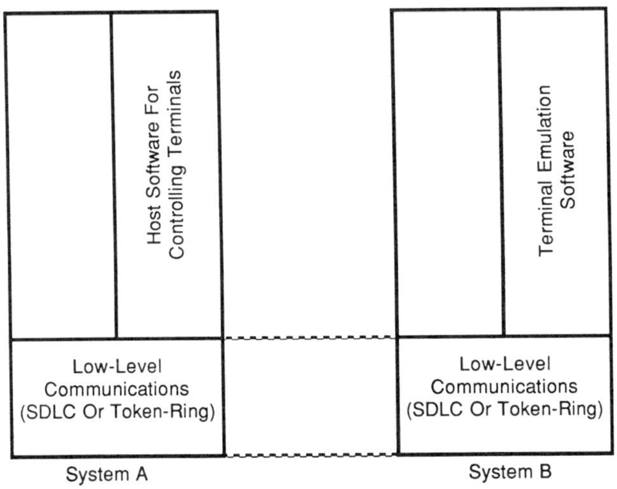

Figure 1-9: Low-Level Communications, Terminal Emulation

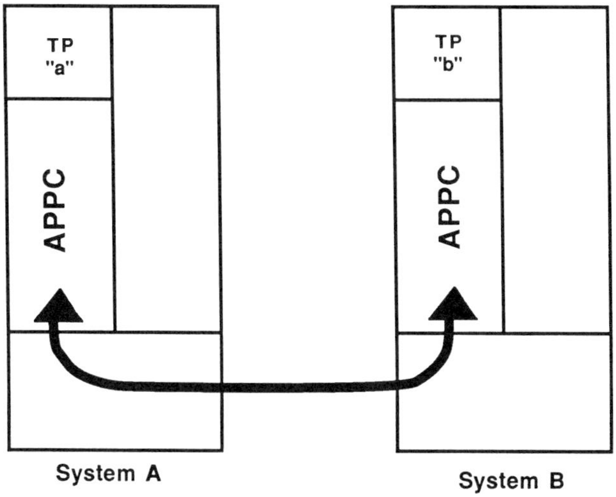

Figure 1-10: Program-to-Program Communication Via APPC

Problem: Porting Transaction Processing Software

Another result of differing program-to-program communication interfaces is that transaction processing software can be ported to new hardware systems only with difficulty. In addition to adapting to other differences between the different machines, programmers have to adapt to the communication programming interfaces, too.

Problem: Transferring Information

Without a standard for program-to-program communication, terminal emulation and cluster controller emulation are frequently used to download information from one machine to a dissimilar machine. However, information transferred in this manner is often difficult to use. For example, information transferred from mainframes to microcomputers may be difficult to integrate with microcomputer applications. PC users normally have to run the communications program, write the desired information to disk, get out of the communications program, and then integrate that information into a microcomputer application. The application often is not designed to accept information from a different machine, a different operating system, or different applications with different file structures.

Excluding unwanted information can be difficult, when the only capture techniques offered are "screen capture" (writing everything on the screen to disk) and file transfer. Frequently, screens and files contain more information than is desired. Also, is the information is not always in the correct format.

Terminal emulation software is often limited in the services it can provide. For example, a host may assume that a terminal has a very limited ability to recover from errors, or to continue in spite of errors. Thus, the terminal emulation software has difficulty providing error recovery services, because it cannot enlist the host's cooperation.

Although some vendors did address these problems, there were no standards to help them, so their solutions were usually limited as to the environments they would run in.

Solution: APPC

APPC provides a standard program-to-program communication interface, independent of operating systems, hardware, programming languages, data formats, communication protocols, and network configurations. Because of this flexibility, APPC has the potential to be implemented almost universally in the data communications world. In theory, APPC could provide universal interconnection for all systems, where appropriate low-level communication links exist. In practice, vendors with non-SNA networking strategies can interconnect their own machines more easily without APPC, and will use APPC for gateways into SNA networks. (See Figure 1-11.) Such gateways have the potential for providing very wide interconnection, either through an SNA network, or simply gateway-to-gateway. (See Figure 1-12.)

Because APPC is designed to be ported to new machines and operating systems, software vendors may be able to implement their programs economically on a wider variety of machines. Users, in turn, may be able to migrate to new hardware systems without having to learn to use new software.

With APPC, the communications link becomes a flexible tool, under the direct control of the application. An application on one machine captures only the desired information, and sends it to an application on another machine in the desired format. This is a "clean" implementation. The applications are designed to work with one another and with the communications link. Figure 1-13 shows the difference between application-to-application information transfer and file-transfer or screen capture.

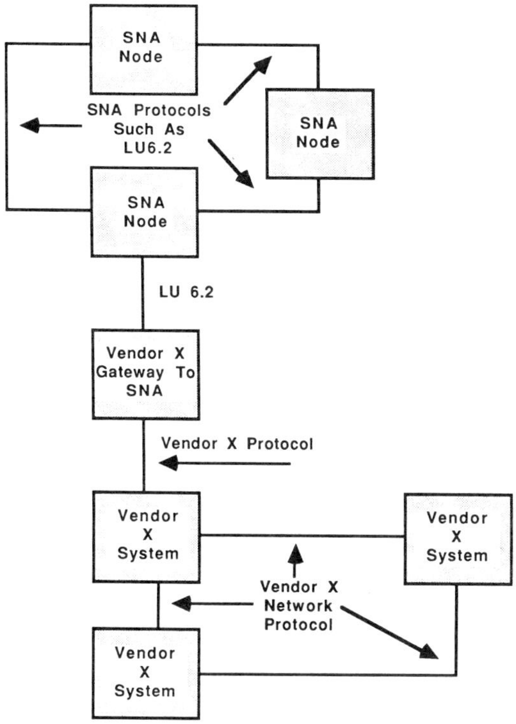

Figure 1-11: LU6.2-Based SNA Gateway

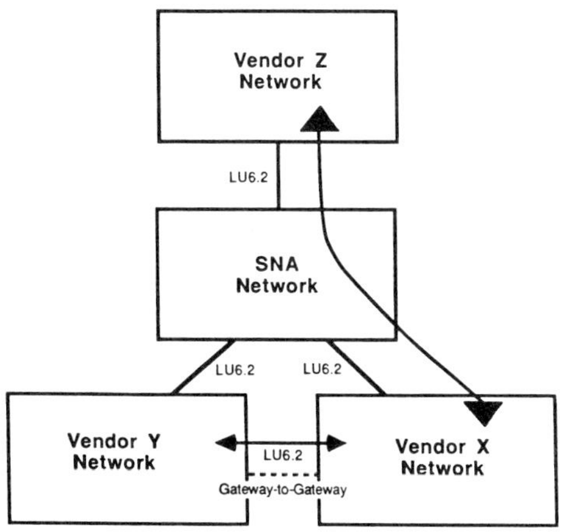

Figure 1-12: SNA Linkage Of Non-IBM Vendors

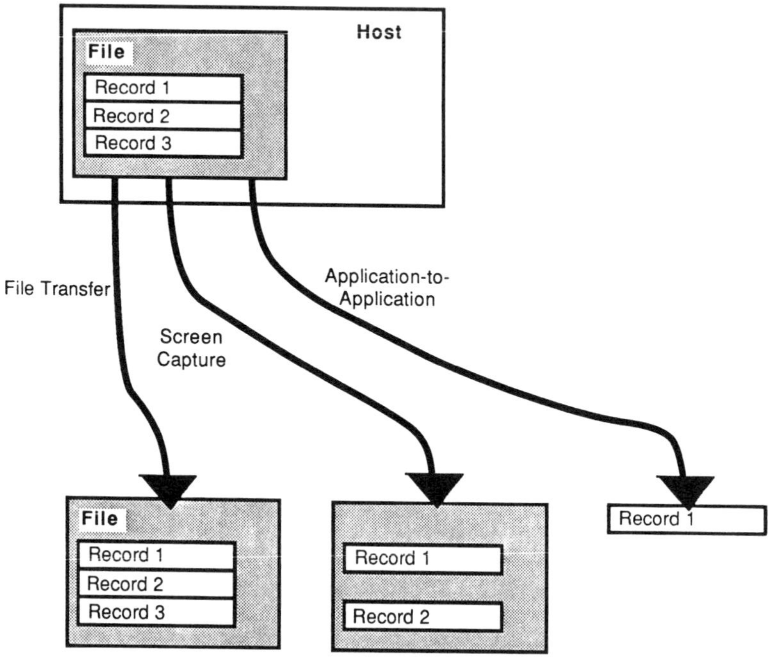

Figure 1-13: Single-Record Transfer Via APPC

APPC offers a rich set of services to application programs: security passwords, error recovery, and management of logical connections, for example. APPC is designed to support sophisticated applications on powerful computers; it offers services appropriate to this environment.

APPC supports the move from terminal emulation to peer-to-peer functionality. For example, APPC is a standard means for a program in a PC to control a program running in a mainframe. This means that users in the SNA environment can exploit the power of their PCs more fully. PCs can cooperate with each other and with other types of computers to perform distributed transaction processing, or simpler types of applications.

1.9 Supported Architectures and Products

LU6.2 was released for CICS systems (Customer Information Control System, a mainframe teleprocessing monitor) in 1982, with Version 1 Release 6 of CICS. In March 1986, LU6.2 was released for the personal computer as APPC/PC. LU6.2 became available for the System/38 in Release 5 of the operating system, and for the

System/36 in Release 8. Support has been announced for the RT (Reduced Instruction Set Computer Technology) PC, Scanmaster I (an image transfer system), Series/1 minicomputer, Displaywriter word processing system (in the Electronic Document Distribution licensed program, no longer being sold effective June 1986), 5520 word processing system, 3820 Page Printer (in the Print Services Facility and the PrintManager), 8100 Distributed Office System (in DPPX, Distributed Processing Program Executive), BusinessView, and the System/88 fault tolerant computer. Thus, LU6.2 will be available on a wide variety of IBM products.

In addition, most other major computer manufacturers are expected to offer LU6.2 compatibility. (See section 3.5.)

One important set of IBM architectures and software products which use LU6.2 today are those associated with DISOSS (Distributed Office Support System). This includes SNA Distribution Services (SNADS), an architecture allowing store-and-forward document distribution between multiple mainframes running DISOSS. Machines submit documents to DISOSS using Document Interchange Architecture (DIA), which defines the rules and data structures for document interchange. DIA is based on LU6.2 in most IBM products. (See sections 3.4, 5.6, 5.7, and 5.8 for more on DIA and SNADS.) DCA (Document Content Architecture) defines formats for documents; it is typically used with DIA but does not itself define communications-related functions. The IBM "Personal Services" mail-management system is a major IBM product which uses DIA and DISOSS facilities. Personal Services is offered for the personal computer line, the System/36, the System/38, and mainframes such as System/370, 4341, 4361, 4381, and 30XX.

Another IBM architecture using LU6.2 is the Distributed Data Management (DDM) architecture. This architecture allows applications to access files without knowing, or needing to know, where those files reside. DDM keeps a list of file locations and automatically sets up access to remote files.

ROLM's Call Detail Collector application, which collects call detail records from telephone switches, can then forward those records to a host computer using DDM and LU6.2. The Call Detail Collector is a NetView/PC application. NetView is IBM's centralized network management system, covering mainframes, minicomputers, telephone switches, and Token Ring LANs. All NetView applications will ultimately use LU6.2.

1.10 Directions

APPC represents a significant step forward in the quest for shared, transparent, "any-to-any" links. APPC will allow micros and minis to take on increasingly important tasks, because of their ability to cooperate with one another and with mainframes. It will tend to erode the boundaries between the MIS department and the end-user, and between the "mainframe world," the "mini world," and the "micro world."

With advances in microcomputer, minicomputer, mainframe, and networking hardware and software, the potential benefits of APPC increase. Users can look forward to powerful distributed transaction processing systems encompassing dissimilar machines, operating systems, system software, and communications links, from multiple vendors.

Such systems will not come quickly, however. Nor will APPC be the only way of achieving them.

1.11 Alternatives

For "IBM shops," as for vendors selling IBM-compatible mainframe hardware and software, there are few likely alternatives to SNADS and APPC for bringing cohesion to fragmented data processing systems. Because of this, even in mixed environments, other vendors or third parties will usually provide gateways into SNADS.

However, a developing alternative to SNADS/APPC/SNA is the Open Systems Interconnection (OSI) model proposed by the International Organization for Standardization (ISO). OSI is designed to provide a service similar to that of APPC and SNA, providing flexible and universal connections between dissimilar systems right up to the program level. OSI will eventually offer an equivalent to LU6.2. Today, the ISO/OSI model is neither complete nor mature. Most estimates are that it is several years away, at least, from offering an alternative to APPC.

Nevertheless, the forces behind OSI are strong, and it appears that OSI will offer a viable alternative to APPC and SNA. Even IBM offers support for certain parts of OSI, and is evaluating expanding this support.

1.12 Timeframe

Most existing code is written for the terminal-to-host environment, or for the PC environment. Very little is designed for a distributed transaction environment.

Distributed transaction programming with LU6.2 is complex, and requires expertise which is rare and expensive today. Thus, LU6.2 will make slow, steady gains, rather than taking the world by storm.

The widest immediate markets for LU6.2 software would appear to be for gateways into SNA from other systems, and for system software such as DDM, which allows existing applications to use LU6.2 indirectly. Direct use of LU6.2 -- requiring heavy modification of current software or development of new applications -- will grow more slowly.

Complexity

SNA is a complex architecture. Distributed transaction processing is a complex type of application. IBM has tried to shelter APPC users from these complexities. For example, because APPC is "subsettable," a given implementation can omit many functions. Furthermore, a programmer can choose to use only certain functions, while retaining the ability to run on and communicate with all LU6.2 implementations. APPC also insulates programmers from lower-level protocols. Finally, APPC is designed to be accessible from high-level programming languages.

Nevertheless, learning to program with APPC is much like learning an entirely new programming language. There are many verbs, parameters, variables, return codes, and options to deal with. Programmers proficient in the use of APPC are a great rarity at this writing. They may continue to be so for some time to come. This is likely to slow the development of APPC-based applications.

Demand for Resources

APPC's complexity may, in turn, be reflected in the resources it demands at the machines where it runs. IBM's APPC/PC, for example, requires about 200 Kbytes of memory, almost a third of the 640-Kbyte maximum typically available with DOS. Figure 1-14 gives APPC/PC memory requirements quoted at an IBM Token Ring technical seminar. However, memory requirements of 214 Kbytes have been noted for all APPC/PC code, not including DOS, software for low-level communication protocols (Token-Ring, in this case), the "application subsystem" program, or the application transaction program. Complex protocols can be expected to require a lot of processing power in order to run efficiently as well. APPC's demands for memory and processing power may slow its acceptance in some environments.

Dissimilar Machines

APPC provides a standard communication interface for applications running on dissimilar machines. However, differences between machines, operating systems,

APPC/PC Base Code	*158K*
IBM Token-Ring Network Adapter Handler	*14K*
SDLC Code	*11K*
APPC/PC Menu-Assigned Workspace	
SDLC Only	*18K*
Token-Ring Only	*21K*
For Each Additional LU	*4.5K*
If Host Connected	*5.5K*
For Each Additional Concurrent Conversation/Session	*2.5K*

Figure 1-14: APPC/PC Memory Requirements

and applications may slow the process of developing distributed transaction programs.

For example, in the microcomputer world, software vendors are not talking about interfacing existing applications to APPC. In addition to the technical difficulties involved on the micro side, a "partner transaction program" would be required on the remote machine. If the remote machine is not a PC, the micro software vendor may have to venture into a new and more complex programming environment. (And, if remote machines are limited to PCs, it is questionable whether it is worth the trouble to interface the application to APPC.)

Generic services could be developed, allowing PCs to share disk space or printers on mainframes, for instance. This is a different matter, however, from allowing an existing spreadsheet program to download a chosen chunk of information from the mainframe or minicomputer, or upload information to the mainframe or mini. The latter requires much more than just a communication interface like APPC; it requires compatibility between PC and mainframe programs, or else a translation capability at the application level.

Limited Upward Compatibility for Mainframe Software

In the mainframe world, applications written for LU6.1 will run under LU6.2. There is also migration support for LU6.0. Most other applications would require significant revision to use APPC.

The first uses of LU6.2 will be for gateways into existing IBM mainframe architectures such as SNADS (SNA Distribution Services) and DIA (Document Interchange Architecture), and for architectures like DDM which do not require modification of existing applications.

1.13 Systems Application Architecture (SAA)

Systems Application Architecture (SAA) is a set of interfaces and protocols developed by IBM, and designed to be used by applications running under different operating systems and in different hardware environments. SAA provides a standard which may help software developers develop applications which can be ported easily from one system to another. Thus, SAA may help APPC programmers overcome some of the difficulties mentioned in the previous section.

Chapter 2 - LU6.2 Basics

Transaction program conversations
Transaction program states
Data exchange and synchronization
Basic functions of LU6.2
LU6.2 verbs, parameters, arguments
Services provided to programs by LU6.2
The role and benefits of Physical Unit 2.1

2.1 Conversations

LUs communicate over logical connections called "sessions." When a program wishes to communicate with another program, it asks the LU for temporary, exclusive use of a session. Many transaction programs may take turns using a single session. Thus, they are said to share a session "serially," or to "time-slice" the session. Each time-slice is called a "conversation." The advantage of this system is that many conversations can be allocated and deallocated without establishing and tearing down multiple sessions, a time- consuming procedure.

Figure 2-1 shows time-slicing. Figure 2-2 shows how the session supports the conversation. Transactions programs normally see only conversations, as shown in Figure 2-2; they are not generally concerned with sessions.

Figure 2-1: Time-Slicing A Session

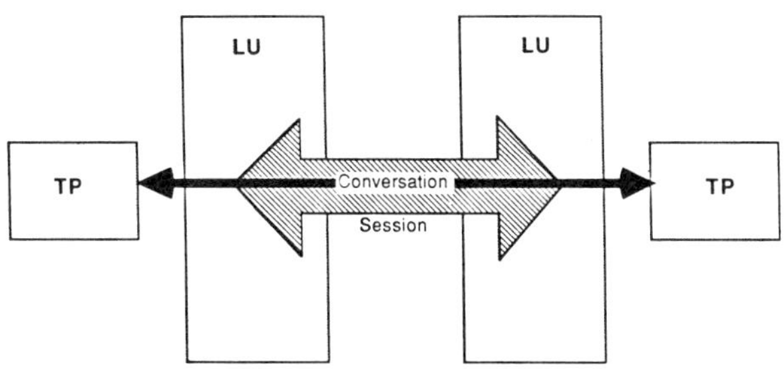

Figure 2-2: Session/Conversation Support

A session is usually a relatively long-term connection, while a conversation is often much shorter. The only real design constraint, however, is that the conversation can never outlast the session.

There are two types of conversations: basic and mapped. These are two different programming interfaces into the LU. The basic conversation inter- face is more flexible and offers more features, but it is also more difficult to use. It is typically used by SNA-defined "service" programs which provide services for other programs. (Chapter 5 discusses these service programs in more detail.)

End-user programs, or programs which are the final users of data exchanged, normally use the mapped conversation interface. When this interface is used, the LU automatically ensures conformance to certain formats and protocols. Thus, the end-user program does not have to concern itself with these matters.

Mapped conversations are intended for user programs communicating with other user programs. Some products (such as printers) which are not intended to run user programs, may support LU6.2, but not mapped conversations. End- user programs can talk to such products using basic conversations.

Two functions available in the mapped interface but not in the basic interface are data stream handling and data mapping. The LU puts all data into a standard data stream format called the "General Data Stream" (GDS), when mapped conversations are used. To do this, the LU forms "GDS variables" by prefixing to the data a length field (called the "LL" field) and an ID field describing the type of GDS record which follows, whether a command or application data. The LL and ID fields are stripped off by the LU on the other end, so that the transaction program does not have to deal with them.

Using the basic interface, the transaction programs on both ends have to insert and strip off the LL and ID fields. GDS is discussed further in sections 4.6 and 4.9.

Mapped and basic conversations are discussed further in section 4.6.

2.2 States

At any given moment, a conversation is in one of four states: reset, send, receive, or confirm. The state applies to the conversation, as seen by the transaction program. For example, for one transaction program, the conversation may be in receive state, while for the partner transaction program, the conversation is in send state.

The state determines what the transaction program can do. For example, when the conversation is in receive state, the program can only receive data. In send state, the program can send data, request confirmation that data was received, and deallocate the conversation. In confirm state, the program can only reply to a confirmation request. Finally, in reset state, the conversation has been destroyed.

2.3 Data Exchange and Synchronization

Only one partner in a conversation can send at a time. When the sending program is finished sending, it relinquishes to the other program the right to send. (See Chapter 6 for programming examples showing exactly how this is done.)

Data and other information sent or received by the LU is stored in buffers in memory. The LU "flushes" its send buffer (sends data) under a number of conditions, including the following: 1) When it cannot accumulate any more data without exceeding the maximum amount it is allowed to transmit in one "request/response unit" (RU) over the session. The RU is the basic unit of data transfer over the session. 2) When the transaction program specifically instructs the LU to send data.

The LU automatically accumulates received data in its receive buffer. When the transaction program "receives" data, it is actually moving data from the LU's receive buffer to the transaction program's receive buffer -- both areas in local memory.

The LU can be instructed to execute a particular section of code, called a "post routine," when information is available to be received. The post routine may contain the program's "receive" request. Thus, the LU receives information and then runs the post routine, which moves that information into another area of memory, leaving the LU free to receive more information.

Two programs can periodically synchronize their activities. There are three possible levels of synchronization. The first is "none." This means exactly what it says. The second is "confirm," which allows programs to send messages confirming that data has been successfully received and processed. Alternatively, they may send error messages indicating information has not been received or successfully processed.

The final, and most sophisticated, type of synchronization is "sync point." This allows two programs to establish "synchronization points" in their processing. A sync point is a certain point in processing. After a sync point is determined, both programs keep "looking backwards," as it were, making plans to return to the sync point, if necessary. At any time, the transaction programs can agree to make permanent all changes which have occurred since a given sync point, or to backtrack, abandoning all changes made since that point. In case of a failure, the

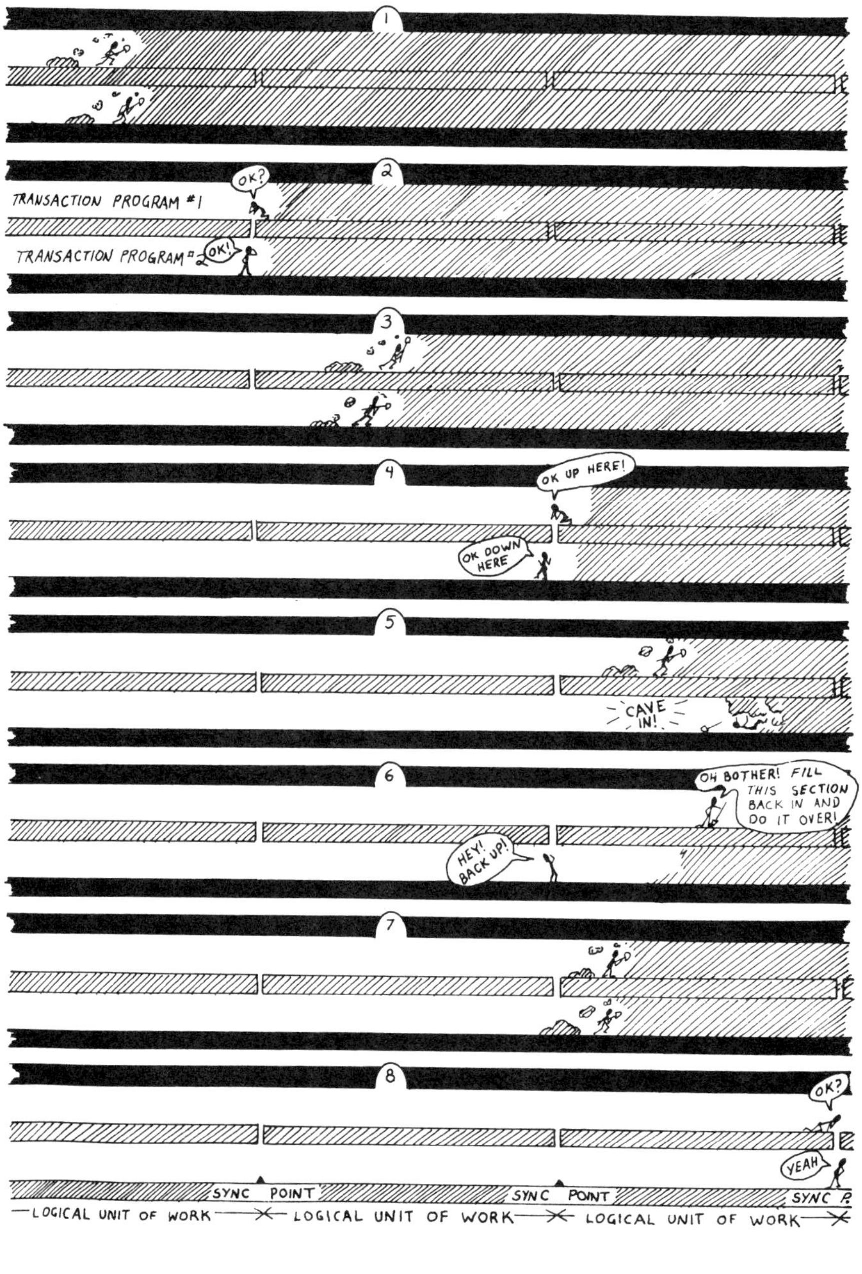

Figure 2-3: Synchronization During Data Exchange

programs return to the most recently defined sync point. Thus, after a failure, the programs would always agree on the status of a sync point-protected database, for example. (See Figure 2-3.)

2.4 Basic Functions

APPC performs twelve basic functions:

Allocate a conversation: asks the local LU to start a conversation with a transaction program in a partner LU.

Send data: places data in the LU's send buffer.

Force send: forces the local LU to send any data in its send buffer.

Receive data: receives data into the program's receive buffer.

Request permission to send: asks permission from the partner program to send data.

Grant permission to send: gives permission to the partner program to send data.

Request confirmation: asks the partner program to confirm that all data has been received and processed successfully.

Accept or reject confirmation: confirms or denies that all data has been received and processed successfully.

Request to be posted when information is available: asks the LU to run a particular post routine when the conversation has information available to be received.

Report an error: reports that an error has occurred.

Obtain conversation attributes: gets the attributes of a conversation, including names of local and partner LUs, type of conversation (basic or mapped), type of confirmation protocols (none, confirm, sync point), and the session's "mode name" (an identifier, created by system definition personnel or control operators, and used by the transaction program and the LU to specify the characteristics of the session, such as "interactive" or "batch," for example).

Deallocate a conversation: ends a conversation.

Chapter 6 provides programming examples which illustrate some of these functions.

2.5 Verbs, Parameters, Arguments

Programming with APPC is accomplished through a set of "verbs." Each verb accomplishes one function. (In some cases a single verb can accomplish more than one function. An example is the RECEIVE_AND_WAIT verb in Figure 6-2.)

An APPC program is essentially a list of verbs to be executed in order by the LU. Other program statements (such as normal Assembly language statements, if the program is in Assembly language) may be included between the verbs. After the transaction program issues each verb, its processing is suspended, while the LU executes the verb (unless the verb completes immediately). The LU then returns control to the program, which may issue another verb or continue with other actions.

The APPC verbs, and the rules which govern them, form the APPC "protocol boundary," the APPC interface as seen by the transaction program.

Each verb may be accompanied by parameters which provide information necessary for carrying out the function. Some parameters may be omitted, while others are required. Some verbs have no parameters.

A parameter may be accompanied by one or more arguments which supply information relating to that parameter. An argument value may be either a "keyword" which is determined by APPC and cannot be changed by the program, or a "variable" which is defined by the program.

Parameters are classified as "supplied parameters" (argument values are supplied by the program when it issues the verb), "supplied-and-returned parameters" (argument values are supplied by the program, but different values may be returned by the LU to the program when the program resumes processing), or "returned parameters" (argument values are returned to the program when it resumes processing).

A verb, with its parameters and their arguments, may be laid out in a "format box" as shown in Figure 2-4. Bracketed parameters are optional. Default argument values are underlined.

2.6 Services Provided to Programs

APPC provides a number of services to transaction programs, in order to allow communication to proceed efficiently, reliably, and securely. These include:

Verb-name	***Supplied Parameters:*** ***Parameter (Argument)*** ***Parameter (Argument)*** ***(Argument)*** ***Parameter (Argument Argument ... Argument)*** ***[Parameter (Argument)]*** ***[Parameter (Default-Argument)]*** ***(Argument)***
	Supplied-and-Returned Parameters: ***Parameter (Argument)***
	Returned Parameters: ***Parameter (Argument)*** ***[Parameter (Argument)]***
	;

Figure 2-4: Format Box, Verbs and Rules

Naming: A name is a character string associated with a particular resource at a particular installation. Each LU can also have "local aliases" for remote resources, so that local transaction programs don't have to keep track of name changes elsewhere in the network. A local control operator does have to maintain "name translation" tables.

Two-way alternate data transfer: Data flows in only one direction at a time. Programming "half-duplex" communication of this sort is easier and less prone to error than programming "full-duplex" communication, in which either side may send at any time.

Simultaneous activation: When a transaction program makes a request of a partner program, the receiving LU will activate that partner program if it is not already active. This is necessary, since many distributed applications require partner programs to be active simultaneously.

Overhead management: Numerous small messages use communication lines less efficiently than a smaller number of large messages. APPC attempts to send the maximum possible amount of data in each RU. (See Chapter 6 for examples.)

Attention request: Programs have access to an "attention" mechanism, through which they can, for example, request the right to send when they are in receive state.

Commitment control: The sync point function allows programs to commit to, or refrain from committing to, changes in protected resources.

Symmetrical communication: One active program allocates and defines certain aspects of a conversation. All other functions (data transfer, attention request and response, error notification, and deallocation) may be performed by either partner program.

Primary and secondary LUs: The LU that activates a session is called the "primary LU." The other LU connected to the session is the "secondary LU." The primary LU always has the right to initiate the first conversation on the session. (The primary LU will be the "contention winner" if both LUs try to initiate a conversation at the same time.) Generally, every LU6.2 implementation can be either the primary or the secondary LU. This is one aspect of the symmetrical, peer-to-peer design of LU6.2.

Mode of service definition: The allocating program determines the mode of service, such as "interactive" or "batch," required by the conversation.

Conversation typing: Mapped and basic conversations are provided.

Subset definition: See section 4.8.

Session sharing: APPC automatically shares sessions among conversations.

Security: The LU provides an optional function set consisting of three security functions: partner LU verification, partner end-user verification, and session encryption. Each pair of LUs may establish a password which they use in establishing sessions. When an "end-user" (which in LU6.2 is a transaction program) requests access to another transaction program, it may be required to provide a user ID and password. Session encryption or cryptography permits all data to be encrypted at the source LU and decrypted at the target LU; between the two LUs, it is not comprehensible.

Parallel Sessions: Each session can only support one conversation at a time. When two LUs require multiple simultaneous conversations, the conversations must be supported by multiple simultaneous sessions. Multiple LUs are not required, however. Multiple sessions between the same two LUs are called "parallel sessions." In Figure 1-4, for example, two of the three LUs have parallel sessions. Parallel session capability is an important part of LU6.2. However, not all LU6.2 products support it. Some products (a printer, for example) may be inherently single-tasking and unable to handle multiple simultaneous sessions.

Error Handling: Errors are handled through confirmation, sync point, program error indication, and abnormal conversation deallocation. The first two have already been covered. Program error indication allows programs to notify one another when they detect an error. Abnormal conversation deallocation allows a transaction program to terminate a conversation when it detects an unrecoverable error; the partner LU informs the partner TP of the abnormal deallocation.

2.7 PU2.1

PU2.1 is a new improved SNA physical unit type, supporting Type 2 peripheral nodes. PU2.1 is required to allow all PU2.1 nodes to set up sessions without mediation by a host, and to run multiple sessions simultaneously.

Type 2 nodes are typically cluster controllers in the 3270 family or the 3600 family. PU2.1 supersedes PU2.0, which offers a subset of PU2.1 functions. PU2.1 improves on PU2.0 in two areas: physical connectivity and session support.

In the area of physical connectivity, PU2.1 offers a "direct" connection which PU2.0 does not offer, as well as the "peripheral node" type of connection which is also offered by PU2.0. A direct connection is one made with another PU2.1 node. This is a "peer-coupled" connection. It is not mediated by any other node. Alternatively, the PU2.1 node may act as a peripheral node to a "subarea node." The subarea node is either a host (Type 5) node, or a communication controller (Type 4) node. The subarea node provides "boundary function" support such as the Network Control Program (NCP). The difference between the "direct" and "peripheral node" connections is seen at session initiation and termination. The direct connection requires no central control point to handle session services. The peripheral node connection requires one or more System Services Control Points (SSCPs) which initiate and terminate all sessions.

In the area of session support, PU2.1 supports primary LU capability, multiple sessions, and parallel sessions. These have all been discussed above.

Chapter 3 - LU6.2-Compatible Products

Low-Level Communication Protocols
Devices (computers, Scanmaster, Displaywriter ...)
Application Services (DIA, DCA, SNADS)
Distributed Office Support System (DISOSS)

3.1 Low-Level Communication Protocols

LU6.2 requires some type of data link. SDLC (Synchronous Data Link Control) communication products are, in general, LU6.2-compatible in that they are capable of providing that link. A Token Ring network can also provide the data link for APPC. Figure 3-1 shows how these products provide a data link connection for APPC.

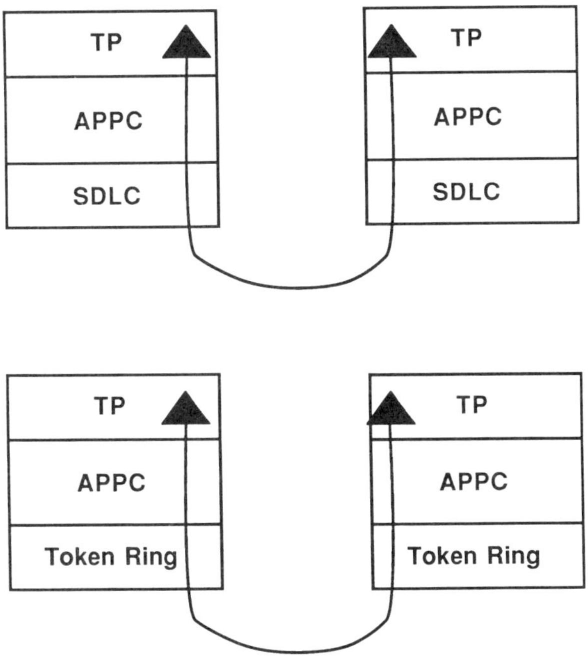

Figure 3-1: SDLC, Token-Ring Support of APPC

3.2 IBM Devices

IBM devices for which LU6.2 implementations have been announced include:

IBM mainframes (under CICS)
IBM PC/XT/AT
RT-PC
System/38 (in Release 8)
System/36 (in Release 5)
Series/1
Scanmaster I
Displaywriter word processing system
5520 word processing system
3820 Page Printer
8100 Distributed Office System
System/88 fault tolerant computer

The System/38 implements a T2.1 node and LU6.2. Release 5 of the Control Program Facility is required, as are Vertical Microcode extensions. The S/38 LU6.2 implementation supports a number of optional LU6.2 functions. Among them is the mapped conversation applications programming interface (API). Thus, the S/38 is an "open box": users can write programs to its LU6.2. Refer to the System/38 Data Communications Programmers Guide for more information.

The Electronic Document Distribution (EDD) licensed program for the Displaywriter implements a T2.1 node and a single LU6.2. (IBM ceased selling this product in June of 1986.)

3.3 IBM Software Products

DISOSS, SNADS, and DIA

One group of IBM software products which use LU6.2 are those associated with DISOSS (Distributed Office Support System). This includes SNA Distribution Services (SNADS), an architecture allowing store-and-forward document distribution between networked mainframes running DISOSS. Machines submitting documents to DISOSS use Document Interchange Architecture (DIA), which defines the rules and data structures for document interchange. SNADS always uses LU6.2. DIA is based on LU6.2 in most IBM products. SNADS is discussed in section 5.6. DIA is discussed in section 5.7. Their interworking is discussed in section 5.8.

Personal Services

Personal services is an IBM application which provides office system functions. It supports the Displaywrite word processing package, electronic mail, document distribution, library services, and printing. Personal Services transfers information using DIA, SNADS, and DISOSS.

Personal Services/370 runs on mainframes with either the MVS or VSE operating systems, and CICS/VS and DISOSS/370. (See section 1.9 for a list of mainframes which support Personal Services/370.)

Personal Services/38 (for the IBM System/38 minicomputer) is part of the System/38 OFFICE/38 series of programs. The System/38 Control Program Facility (CPF) is the primary interface to System/38 system functions, including SNADS and DIA. Thus, it is through the CPF that the System/38 supports LU6.2. Documents can be exchanged, using SNADS, with the System/36, System/38, DISOSS/370, and 5520 word processor.

Personal Services/36 (for the IBM System/36 minicomputer) allows users to distribute documents to other System/36 users (using DIA), DISOSS users via DISOSS/370 (using DIA and SNADS), a Displaywriter user via Electronic Document Distribution (EDD), a 5520 via 5520 Administrative Processing Program (APP), and the 8100 Distributed Office System, through the Distributed Processing Program Executive (DPPX). All are based on LU6.2.

Personal Services/PC supports both PC-to-PC and PC-to-mainframe communication. The PC-to-mainframe connection uses DIA to talk to DISOSS. DISOSS will then use SNADS if necessary, to forward the document to another DISOSS node. Personal Services/PC uses LU2 and LU1 (Network Terminal Option) rather than LU6.2.

Distributed Data Management (DDM)

Distributed Data Management (DDM) is an IBM architecture using LU6.2. DDM allows applications to access files without knowing, or needing to know, where those files reside. DDM support is integrated into the operating system. When a request for a file is made, the operating system searches the local disk directory first. If it does not find the file, DDM searches the Network Resource Directory, a list of files and their locations. If it finds the file there, DDM automatically sets up access to the remote file, using LU6.2. DDM support has been announced for the System/36, System/38, and CICS. Figure 3-2 illustrates the functioning of DDM.

Figure 3-2: DDM Functionality

ROLM Call Detail Collector

ROLM's Call Detail Collector application, which collects call detail records from telephone switches, can then forward those records to a host computer using DDM and LU6.2. The Call Detail Collector is a NetView/PC application. NetView is IBM's centralized network management system, covering mainframes, minicomputers, telephone switches, and Token Ring LANs. All NetView applications will ultimately use LU6.2.

Application-to-Application Networking (APPN)

Application-to-Application Networking (APPN) is a Low Entry Networking (LEN) capability based on enhancements to LU6.2 and PU2.1. Its two major features are decentralized routing and dynamic network configuration.

Decentralized routing permits peripheral nodes to perform intermediate routing functions. In a traditional SNA network, subarea nodes such as host mainframes or communication controllers perform intermediate network routing. Peripheral nodes, such as cluster controllers, minicomputers, and personal computers, are dependent on subarea nodes for routing. APPN allows peripheral nodes to perform routing functions, either supplementing the subarea nodes, or replacing them and creating a network which consists entirely of peripheral nodes.

APPN also permits dynamic network configuration. When a new node is added to a traditional SNA network, a system programmer or network operator has to modify statically defined routing tables within the subarea node. This operation is referred to as a SYSGEN. When a new node is added to an APPN network, its address is broadcast to all other nodes on the network. No SYSGEN is required.

A PU2.1 node enhanced for APPN operation is referred to as a Network Node. PU2.1 peripheral nodes can attach to PU2.1 Network Nodes rather than to subarea nodes. A Directory Services facility searches directories, both local and remote, to determine which Network Node houses a desired LU. A Connectivity Services facility in the Network Node maintains a Topology Data Base which helps a route selection service select the best route between two LUs. An LU-to-LU session can then be established.

At this writing, only the System/36 can function as an APPN Network Node.

3.4 Third-Party Devices

Most minicomputer and mainframe manufacturers are expected to offer LU6.2 compatibility, often in the context of a bridge to DISOSS. This section represents information available in late 1986.

In June, 1985, AT&T announced a synchronous communication adapter, the ISC (Intelligent Serial Controller), for its line of 3B minicomputers. The ISC card, with accompanying software, provides SDLC connections, as well as various types of 3270 emulation. AT&T plans an LU6.2 implementation for its 3B2 line of minicomputers. This LU6.2 implementation, due for release in the first quarter of 1987, works in conjunction with the ISC card. No service TPs will be available with the LU initially.

In the Fall of 1985, Digital Equipment Corporation (DEC, of Merrimack, New Hampshire), maker of the VAX, MicroVAX, and Rainbow computers, began offering a "document exchange interconnect capability" which supports both the library and distribution services of DISOSS. This software bridge to DISOSS supports DIA and DCA (revisable and final form documents). The document exchange facility resides on the "DECnet/SNA Gateway" which supports LU6.2. DEC users, using any of several word processing programs, can retrieve and edit documents stored in an IBM DISOSS library. DEC users can also create documents in a DISOSS library. These documents can then be retrieved and edited by users on either IBM or DEC systems. IBM and DEC users can exchange messages as final form documents, creating a multivendor messaging system. DEC also offers an APPC/LU6.2 Programming Interface which allows an application developer to write a transaction program running on a Digital system which will communicate with a transaction program running on an IBM system, using basic verbs.

Data General, the Westboro, Massachusetts, manufacturer of micros and minis, has LU6.2 capability for its entire line of Eclipse MV processors, from the 2000 up to the 20000, running under the AOS/VS (Advanced Operating System/Virtual Storage) or AOS/DVS (Advanced Operating System/Distributed Virtual Storage) operating systems. Data General offers an interface to DISOSS called "Document Exchange Architecture" (DXA) which supports DIA and SNADS, in conjunction with Data General's CEO office automation software. Like Digital, Data General also support DCA final-form and revisable-form documents. CEO DXA implements PU2.1 and LU6.2. CEO DXA users can access DISOSS libraries and exchange documents, messages, and files with DISOSS and SNADS nodes, as well as peer IBM System/36s and 5520 word processing systems. In addition, the "Application Interface LU6.2" (APILU 6.2) allows Data General COBOL, PL/1, FORTRAN, and Macro Assembler programs to use LU6.2 verbs to communicate with other programs.

Unisys (formerly Burroughs and Sperry) is pursuing two paths in relation to LU6.2:

Burroughs announced, in August 1986, a software application to allow its office automation systems to access DISOSS. The product, OFISbridge, is designed for Burroughs' B25 family of microcomputer workstations. It also supports the

XE520, Burroughs' shared resource processor, which is a departmental system. OFISbridge allows documents created under Burroughs' BTOS operating system to be used in the DISOSS environment. OFISbridge uses a BTOS/SNA gateway and a Burroughs implementation of LU6.2 to access the services provided by DISOSS. It offers full adherence to DCA and DIA.

Sperry announced Distributed Systems Services (DSS) in March 1986. DSS is being implemented in two phases. Phase I connected Sperry products, and was available in October, 1986. This did not require LU6.2. Phase II will connect Sperry networks to DISOSS, using LU6.2, through Sperry's Series 1100 and 2200 mainframes, and perhaps through other Sperry hardware. Sperry also plans to support DIA and DCA, as well as SNADS. Sperry implements the DIA OSN on the mainframe.

Hewlett Packard offers an "Office Connect to DISOSS" product which provides a gateway between "HP Desk" and DISOSS using LU6.2. It also provides a DIA capability. There is no open API for this product. It can only be used by HP Desk. An open interface is reportedly under development, but no announcement has been made about availability.

In June, 1986, Wang Laboratories Inc. (Lowell, MA) announced support for LU6.2 for communication between Wang VS minicomputers and IBM hosts. Wang's DISOSS gateway, release 1.5, can exchange messages of up to 256 characters with an IBM host using an LU6.2 implementation running on the VS. Wang also plans to support SNADS. Soft-Switch (King of Prussia, PA) will provide the document conversion software for SNADS.

Datapoint Corp. of San Antonio, Texas, is reportedly working on an LU6.2 implementation for its line of RMS processors.

Prime Computer Inc., of Boston, Massachusetts, is committed to supporting important IBM standards, and is expected to offer LU6.2.

3.5 Third-Party Software Products

Soft-Switch (King of Prussia, PA) offers a SNADS gateway, which is a full implementation of LU6.2. Soft-Switch believes that this is the first third- party implementation of LU6.2 on an IBM host. The Soft-Switch gateway has been installed at a number of user sites, including International Paper Company in New York.

An LU6.2 implementation from Software Research Corporation (SRC) of Natick, Massachusetts, has reportedly been licensed by Lanier Business Products, Inc.,

Honeywell Inc., and Four-Phase Systems, a subsidiary of Motorola Inc.

Systems Strategies Inc. of New York, NY, offers SNA/LU6.2, an LU6.2 implementation which hardware vendors can port to their hardware.

Chapter 4 - LU6.2 Architecture and Formats

4.1 Positioning LU6.2 in the SNA Layers

SNA is a layered architecture, like the Open Systems Interconnection (OSI) model put forth by the International Organization for Standardization (ISO). Both architectures have seven layers, but the layers of the two systems are only roughly equivalent. (See Figure 4-1.)

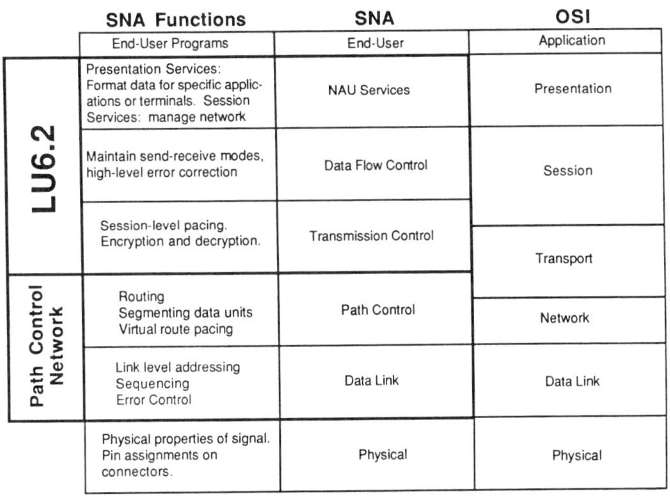

Note: The physical layer is outside SNA

Figure 4-1: SNA, OSI Equivalency

The LU covers the SNA layers between Path Control and Application. The LU receives commands and data from Transaction Programs running at the application layer and passes commands and data to the path control network. In practice, LU6.2 implementations may have to include path control functions. For example, the IBM Token-Ring Network and SDLC both offer a data link interface, so APPC/PC, an LU6.2 implementation which is designed to run on SDLC or the Token Ring, has to provide path control functions. (See Appendix B for more on APPC/PC.)

4.2 Layers and Components of LU6.2

Other than presentation services, the components discussed here are never seen by a programmer or end-user. They constitute the "deep structure" of LU6.2.

End User and NAU Services --

Each LU includes a services manager, which in turn contains an LU network services (LNS) component and a resources manager (RM) component. The components interact as shown in Figure 4-2. When a transaction program (TP) starts, the RM initializes a "half-session" (HS), so called because a session is shared, and half of the session may be considered to reside in each LU. The RM also creates a presentation services (PS) process to service the TP. A separate PS process is spawned to service each instance of each TP. The RM then assigns the HS to the PS process. Thereafter, data flow is directly between the HS and PS. RM "gets out of the way" after it sets up the connection.

The TP then begins to issue LU6.2 verbs requesting LU services. For example, a TP might issue the "ALLOCATE" verb to allocate a session with a remote LU and establish a conversation with a remote TP. The PS process receives verbs, checks that each verb is valid in the current conversation state, processes and translates verbs when necessary (as when mapped conversations are used), and routes valid verbs to the HS.

Data Flow Control and Transmission Control --

The half-session has four major components: an initializer (to activate the half-session), a router (to distribute messages to the data flow control and transmission control components), a data flow control component (to handle certain aspects of data traffic flow), and a transmission control component (which handles data exchange between the data flow control component and the path control network).

Message units received from path control (PC) are routed to transmission control (TC), which passes them up to data flow control (DFC). Message units received from LNS, RM, and PS are passed to DFC. DFC passes them down to TC, which

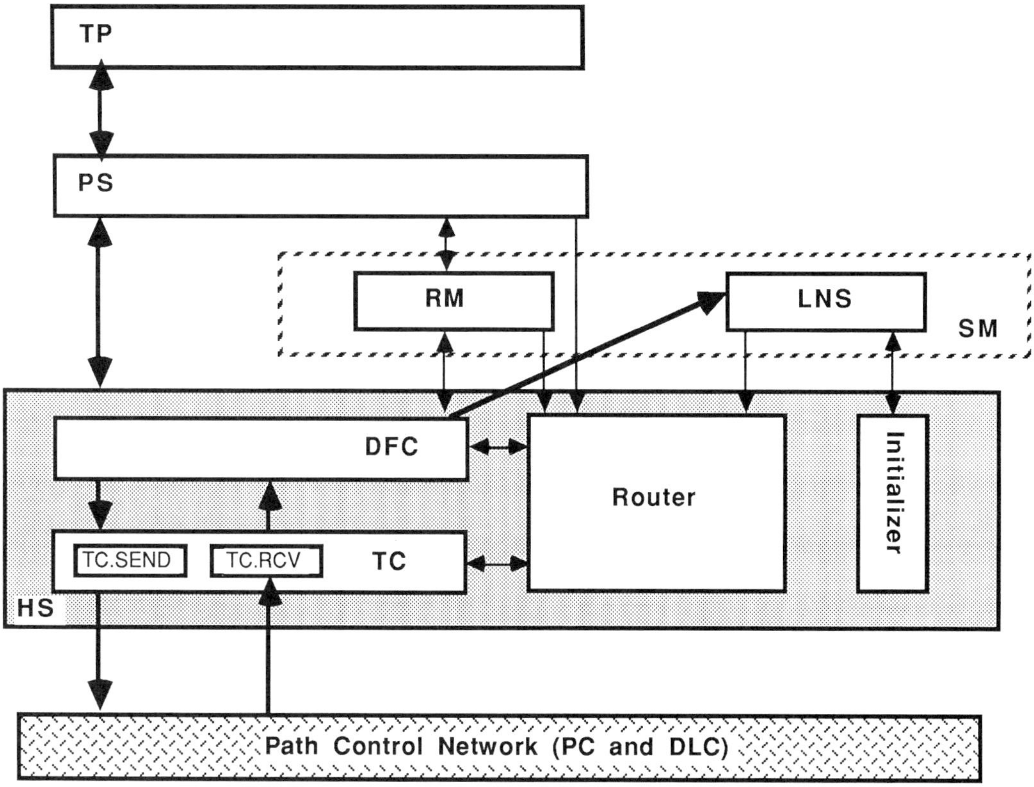

(Dark Arrows Show Main Data Path)

TP = Transaction Program
PS = Presentation Services
RM = Resources Manager
LNS = LU Network Services
DFC = Data Flow Control
TC = Transmission Control
HS = Half Session
SM = Services Manager
PC = Path Control
DLC = Data Link Control

Figure 4-2: LU6.2 Layers, Components

forwards them to PC.

Both DFC and TC help ensure that data is exchanged in an orderly manner. DFC mediates between LNS, RM, and PS on the one hand, and HS on the other. DFC keeps track of which end of the session is supposed to talk next, performs some error recovery, and handles data units and structures such as chains of related requests. TC mediates between HS and PC, making sure that message units are received in order, and that neither side sends data too fast for the other.

Path Control Network --

Not a part of the LU, the path control network, consisting of path control (PC) and data link control (DLC) components, takes message units from the local LU and routes them to the remote LU. It also takes message units from the remote LU and routes them to the local LU. The path control network handles all the physical details of routing the message, so that the LUs deal only with logical entities such as sessions.

4.3 The Protocol Boundary: APPC Verbs

Application programmers do not have to deal with the layers and components discussed above. The interface between the TP and PS is the TP-LU "protocol boundary." The protocol boundary consists of a set of verbs. SNA does not define the format or syntax of the verbs. However, it does define the basic set of functions. The APPC verbs are listed in Appendix A.

When a protocol boundary can be used by a user-written program, it becomes an "applications programming interface" (API).

There are two main kinds of APPC verbs, each with three subcategories:

1. conversation verbs

a. mapped conversation verbs
b. basic conversation verbs
c. type-independent conversation verbs

2. control operator verbs.

a. change number of sessions verbs
b. session control verbs
c. LU definition verbs.

The conversation verbs permit program-to-program communication. Figure 4-3 illustrates how basic conversation verbs are used to send data from one TP to another.

```
TP "a"                                   TP "b"
[ TP "a" already running ]
ALLOCATE
      SYNC_LEVEL (NONE)
SEND_DATA

DEALLOCATE     ------------------->     [ TP "b" Starts ]
      TYPE (SYNC_LEVEL)                  RECEIVE_AND_WAIT
[End Conversation ]                      RECEIVE_AND_WAIT
                                         DEALLOCATE
                                               TYPE (LOCAL)
                                         [ End Conversation ]
```

TP "a" issues three verbs to allocate a conversation, send data, and deallocate the conversation. The LU sends all requests and data in one transmission. TP "b" receives data with one "receive" verb, the deallocation request with a second "receive" verb, and then issues a local "deallocate."

Figure 4-3: APPC Basic Conversation Verbs

The control operator verbs permit the "control operator transaction program" to control the LU. A control operator transaction program is an SNA-defined but implementation-specific or installation-specific program that assists a control operator in controlling the LU.

4.4 The Application Subsystem

Certain functions of the LU may be left to each particular installation or product to formalize. This may require a user-written extension to the LU. In APPC/PC, this user-written extension is the "application subsystem." The application subsystem is not mentioned in the LU6.2 architecture definition. However, something of the sort is implied by the fact that certain LU func- tions may be carried out using installation-specified methods.

For example, the LU6.2 architecture prescribes no particular method for determining LU-LU passwords. Products offering the "LU-LU Verification Security" option must offer some means of determining LU-LU passwords. APPC/PC does this in the application subsystem. The LU, through the AC-

CESS_LU_LU_PW command, requests that the application subsystem provide an LU-LU password. ACCESS_LU_LU_PW is an implementation-specific (product-specific) command; it was invented for APPC/PC. The code for creating the passwords is installation-specific; it is written by the application subsystem programmer.

The application subsystem is responsible for checking for incoming "allo- cates," requests to allocate (assign) a conversation to a TP. An incoming allocate may be for any TP at the node. The application subsystem checks for allocates and then loads an instance of the required TP, or allows an existing instance of the TP to receive the verb. The application subsystem uses the GET_ALLOCATE verb, which is defined by APPC/PC but not by LU6.2, to check for incoming allocates.

In general, the architecture assumes that the LU will start a new instance of a TP for each incoming allocate request. This is a simple procedure which does not require a specific verb for checking incoming allocates; a normal "receive" verb will do the job.

However, this standard procedure might place an undue burden on single- tasking DOS, and on personal computers with limited memory. Thus, the APPC/PC LU may have to do something more complex, namely, assign a conversation to an existing TP. APPC/PC provides the product-specific GET_ALLOCATE verb to permit this, by making it possible for the LU to check for incoming allocates without actually "dequeuing" one. This allows APPC/PC to leave allocate requests "on hold" until it is ready to respond to them; this is necessary if conversations are to be assigned to programs that are already running.

There are a number of such product-specific verbs in APPC/PC. Another example is the verb TP_VALID. This verb must be sent by the application subsystem to APPC/PC after the application subsystem validates and loads a new transaction program, and before issuing any conversation verbs for the new TP.

4.5 Conversation Verbs

Figure 4-3 illustrates the use of several conversation verbs.

In the figure, TP "a" issues an ALLOCATE verb. This causes LU "a" to allocate a conversation and places an allocation request for TP "b" in the send buffer. The "synchronization level" of the ALLOCATE verb is "none." This means that TP "b" does not have to confirm that it has received and acted upon information it has received. (Confirmation would not, in any case, occur at this point. See Chapter 6.) The allocation request does not fill the LU's send buffer, so nothing is sent to TP "b."

TP "a" then issues the SEND_DATA verb. The LU places the data in the send buffer. Again, the allocation request plus the data do not fill the LU's send buffer, so nothing is sent to TP "b." (Alternatively, the buffer could be full at this point, causing the LU to transfer the information.)

TP "a" issues a DEALLOCATE. This causes the LU "a" to discard its control information for the conversation, and to place a DEALLOCATE_NORMAL indication in the send buffer. The synchronization level is "sync level," which means the synchronization level of the DEALLOCATE is the same as the synchronization level of the ALLOCATE. In this case, the sync level of the ALLOCATE was "none." Thus, TP "b" will not have to confirm receiving information. LU "a" sends the contents of the send buffer and ends the conversation.

LU "b" receives the allocation request and strips it off. TP "b" receives the data by issuing a RECEIVE_AND_WAIT verb, and the DEALLOCATE_NORMAL indicator by issuing a second RECEIVE_AND_WAIT verb. RECEIVE_AND_WAIT does two things: 1) It causes TP "b" to wait for information to be received. 2) It will also cause the information to be received, when the information arrives. (In this case, the information has already arrived, so there is no waiting.)

TP "b" then issues a local DEALLOCATE, which causes LU "b" to throw away its control information for the conversation.

4.6 Mapped Versus Basic Conversations

There are fourteen mapped and fourteen basic conversation verbs. They perform essentially the same functions. In fact, they are not mutually exclusive alternatives, though they appear to be so to the programmer. (A basic conversation cannot issue mapped verbs, and vice versa.) Rather, mapped conversations are an option available with basic conversations. When the option is supported and selected, PS translates mapped verbs into basic verbs before passing them to the RM.

Mapped and basic conversations are intended for use by different kinds of programs. Mapped conversation verbs are meant to be used by "application transaction programs," that is, transaction programs which accomplish something directly useful to the end-user. Basic conversations are meant to be used by "service transaction programs." The purpose of a service transaction program is to offer a service to an application transaction program. (See section 4.9.) Generally speaking, basic conversations are more flexible, more powerful, and more difficult to use than mapped conversations.

One major difference between mapped and basic conversations is that a "mapping option" may be available for use with mapped conversations. Mapping allows TPs to select transformations, called "maps," to be performed on data at the sending and receiving nodes. The transformations are defined by the TP and performed by the LU. The LU also supports the exchange of "map names" to refer to maps. (For more details, see SNA Format and Protocol Reference Manual for LU6.2, page 2-39.) Not all LU6.2 implementations support mapping, even if they support mapped conversations. APPC/PC does not, for example.

To the programmer, the most obvious difference between mapped and basic conversations is that basic conversations require a header to be sent with each block of data.

When one sends data using a mapped conversation, one sends just a block of data, which is assumed by APPC to be a complete "data record." There is no header, just the program data. PS then maps the data record into a "mapped conversation record" (MCR). (See section 4.9 for more on the data record and the MCR.)

In contrast, every time one sends data using a basic conversation, one has to precede the data with a header field. The header field must contain a two-byte "logical length" (LL) portion, which specifies the length of the "logical record," including the header field itself. The header field may also contain an identification (ID) portion, which specifies the type of data. The ID portion is optional. Together, the LL portion and the ID portion form the "LLID prefix."

Similarly, when one receives data with a basic conversation, one receives the LLID prefix with the data. When one receives data with a mapped conversation, one receives just the data.

A record length field is not required in mapped conversations, because when data is sent in a mapped conversation, APPC assumes that exactly one complete data record is placed in the send buffer each time the "send" verb is issued. Similarly, the mapped conversation "receive" verb receives exactly one data record at a time, no more and no less. The "data record" is application-defined; it consists of whatever the application puts in the send buffer. The LU has no way to know whether the data sent and received constitute a whole record, a partial record, or more than onerecord, to the application programs. The LU simply transfers the data and leaves the rest up to the applications.

As part of mapped-conversation support, presentation services in the LU segments the MCR into "logical records" and concatenates one or more logical records in a General Data Stream (GDS) variable. ("Logical records" and "GDS variables' are defined in section 4.9. See also section 2.1.) Figure 4-4 illustrates the relationship of the data record, the MCR, the logical record, and the GDS variable.

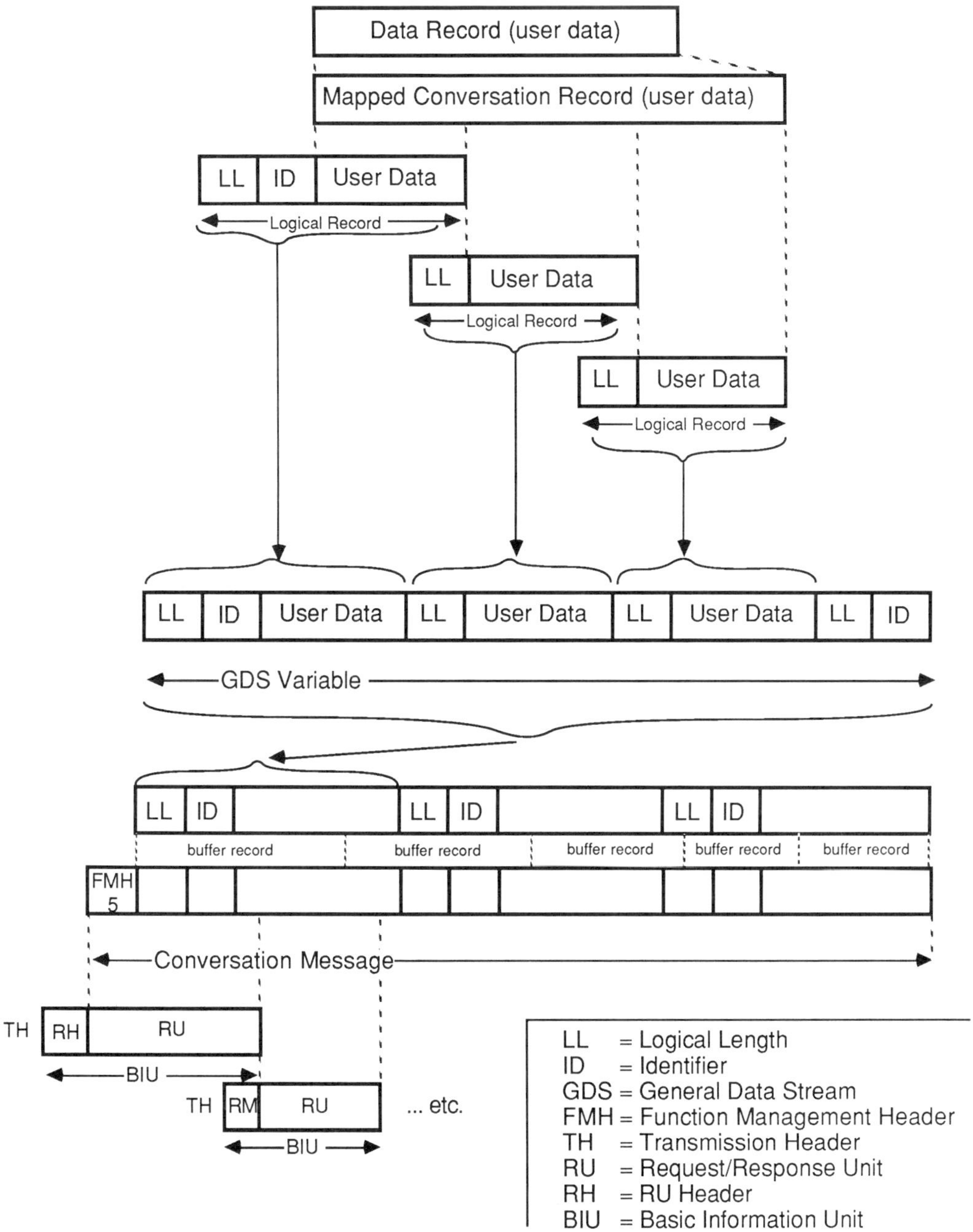

Figure 4-4: Message Units and Their Transformations

With a basic conversation, the send buffer could contain, for example, the end of one logical record, all of the next logical record, and the beginning of a third logical record. Or two complete logical records and the beginning of a third. Or a partial logical record and then four complete logical records. There are no limitations. This allows a program to send information when it is most efficient to do so, rather than when a complete logical record is available.

4.7 Control Verbs

Control verbs do not transfer TP data over communication lines. Rather, they allow a control operator to manipulate certain aspects of the LU or the LU's environment, such as the PU. Eight such verbs are defined by the LU6.2 architecture. Two are used to activate and deactivate a session. Four have to do with setting limits on the number of sessions the LU will support.

The remaining two control verbs are "open-ended" in nature. The LU does not limit the types of data structures upon which they can operate. These are DEFINE and DISPLAY. DEFINE allows the control operator to initialize and modify data structures which the LU maintains to track LUs, partner LUs, modes, TPs, and any other entities which may be important to the LU. DISPLAY displays the information in these data structures.

LU6.2 architecture defines a "control operator transaction program" which issues control operator verbs. In general, control operator verbs have the following types of functions: 1) create and modify data structures that define the LU and the network resources it can access (control points, transaction programs, partner LUs, and modes), 2) activate and deactivate sessions, 3) control numbers of sessions and "contention winner/contention loser" polarities of sessions, and 4) where parallel sessions are supported, to set a limit on the number of parallel sessions permitted between a specific pair of LUs.

For more on "contention winner/contention loser" polarities, see the glossary under "contention," and "Primary and secondary LUs" in section 2.6.

See section 4.9 for more on the control operator TP.

As an example of how control verbs are used, one has but to look at APPC/PC. APPC/PC defines four major functions for control verbs: 1) Define the PU, 2) define local LUs, 3) start local transaction programs, and 4) process asynchronous events detected by the LU, such as incoming "allocate" requests from partner LUs, or information arriving for inclusion in the system log.

Some control verbs are sent by APPC/PC to the application subsystem. Figure 4-5 illustrates the movement of APPC/PC control verbs.

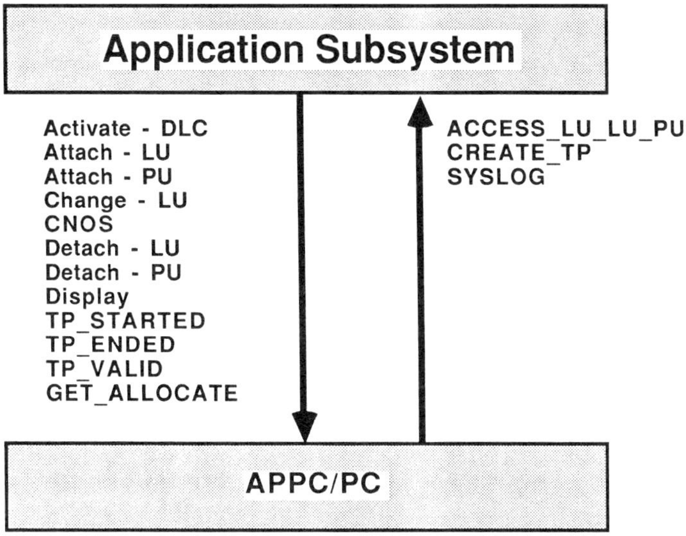

Figure 4-5: Movement of APPC/PC Control Verbs

4.8 Base and Optional Function Sets

LU6.2 is organized into subsets of functions. There are two "base function sets" which all "open API" implementations of the LU must support. In addition, there are a number of "optional function sets," any or all of which may be omitted or included in any given implementation of the LU. However, if an implementation includes any of the functions in an optional function set, it must include all the functions in that set.

All implementations of LU6.2 can communicate with one another. For example, an LU6.2 implementation which includes only the base function sets can communicate with another implementation which includes all the optional function sets. However, none of the options could be used in this case, since one of the implementations would not support them.

The two base functions sets are basic conversations and mapped conversations. All LU implementations with an "open API" (that is, which support arbitrary user-written programs) support both mapped and basic conversations. LU implementations with a "closed API" (that is, not supporting arbitrary user-written programs, but providing only a fixed set of service TPs) do not normally support the mapped conversation option. (See section 4.6 for more on mapped and basic conversations.)

Optional function sets may be divided into five major categories, the first three of which contain only one option set each: 1) mapping, described in section 4.6, 2) sync point, described in section 2.3, 3) program initialization parameters (PIPs), described in this section, 4) security, some aspects of which are described in this section, and 5) performance options, which maximize performance. For example, a performance option might allow a TP to accelerate or eliminate certain types of acknowledgements.

Figure 4-6 shows the LU6.2 base and the five categories of function sets. The figure shows that some options are dependent on other options. For example, transaction security depends on session security.

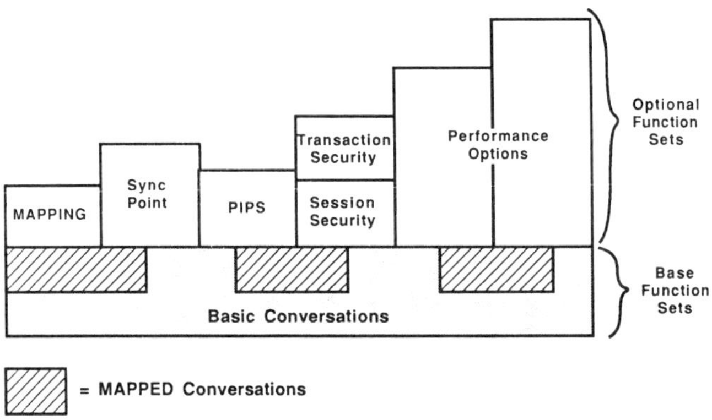

Figure 4-6: Base And Optional Function Sets

Optional functions can also be categorized as "send options" and "receive options." Send options affect the sending LU only. There is no associated option at the receiving LU, because all LU implementations can receive the formats and protocols defined by send options. Receive options, in contrast, define functions which are optional both at the sending and at the receiving LU; both communicating LUs must support a receive option.

Most option sets are send options. For example, all performance options are send options. Receive options have to do with sync point, security, PIP data, mapping, and "function management headers." The receive options are:

Sync point services: described in section 2.3.

User ID verification: verifies that incoming allocate requests should be accepted from a particular user ID.

Program-supplied user ID and password: allows the program allocating a conversation to specify the user ID and password to be sent on the allocation request.

Profile passthrough: allows the program allocating a conversation to instruct the LU to include with the allocation request the profile of the user ID that started the program.

Program-supplied profile: allows the program allocating a conversation to provide the profile included with an allocation request.

PIP data: allows the program allocating a conversation to supply "program initialization parameters" (PIPs) with the allocation request. PIPs are defined and supplied by the application TP. They are not interpreted by the LU.

Data mapping: allows a program to request mapping by local and remote LUs. (See section 4.6.)

FMH data: allows programs to send and receive data records containing "function management header" (FMH) data which is meaningful only to the programs themselves.

4.9 Message Units and Their Transformations

A "message unit" (MU) is a bit-string whose format may be defined by SNA, and which is passed between SNA layers or sublayers. As a message unit is transferred from layer to layer, it changes form. This section describes transformations at the sending LU. Transformations at the receiving LU are exactly reversed.

Figure 4-4 shows the relationships between the various MUs.

Data Record

An application program using a mapped conversation, for example, sends exactly one "data record" each time it issues the MC_SEND_DATA verb. The format of this data record is not defined or limited in any way by the LU6.2 architecture. It can consist of one or many data structures or variables, not necessarily contiguous to one another, and in any format, with any content.

Mapped Conversation Record

The mapped conversation support in the LU first transforms the data record into a "mapped conversation record" (MCR). The MCR differs from the data record at least in that it is a contiguous byte string. It may also have undergone mapping transformations specified by the TP. The MCR contains no information which is used by the LU. It is still strictly a TP-related message unit.

General Data Stream (GDS) Variable

The mapped conversation support then transforms the MCR into a General Data Stream (GDS) variable. A GDS variable consists of a "GDS header" followed by data. The GDS header is the LLID prefix described in sections 2.1 and 4.6. The LL field gives the length of the entire GDS variable, including the LLID prefix.

The GDS format is used by SNA service TPs and by some internal LU components, including mapped conversation support. Application TPs, on the other hand, do not necessarily use the GDS format. This is equivalent to saying that SNA service TPs use basic conversations, while application TPs may use either basic or mapped conversations. The TP using a mapped conversation does not format data as GDS variables, because the mapped conversation support in the LU performs this function.

Logical Record

A "logical record" is an LL prefix followed by data. Within the GDS variable, the TP using the basic conversation can define logical records. Alternatively, the GDS variable may be just one logical record. The logical record is the smallest unit for which the LU detects or reports truncation.

Figure 4-7 shows multiple logical records within a single GDS variable.

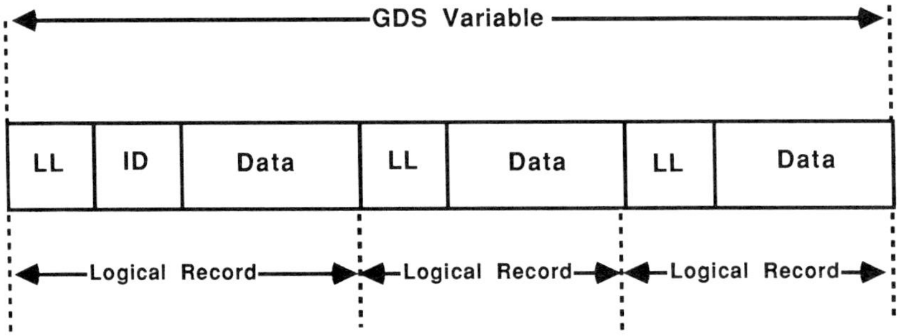

Figure 4-7: Logical Records Within a GDS Variable

Buffer Record

A buffer record is the data in the TP's send or receive buffer when the program issues a basic conversation "send" or "receive" verb. As described in section 4.6, TPs using basic conversations may derive efficiencies from the fact that the buffer record may hold any number of complete or partial logical records. Thus, the program doesn't need to wait to receive a complete logical record before it sends or receives information. It can also send many small logical records with a single verb issuance.

Note, however, that the buffer record is not the message unit which is sent over the transmission line. The "send" verb simply moves information from the TP's send buffer to the LU's buffer. See Chapter 6 for illustrations of this fact.

A receiving TP may optionally direct the LU to begin a new buffer record for each new logical record received.

Conversation Messages

A "conversation message" consists of a sequence of records (logical records for basic conversations, data records for mapped conversations) transferred in one direction from one TP to another without an intervening change of direction or confirmation.

An "ATTACH function management header" (or FMH-5) is considered part of the first basic conversation message. The FMH-5 gives the name and characteris- tics of the target TP. Characteristics include, for example, the option sets required.

Basic Information Unit

The LU breaks the conversation message up into Basic Information Units (BIUs), which is the unit the path control network requires. The BIU consists of a "request/response header" (RH) followed by a "request/response unit" (RU). RHs carry protocol information encoded from TP verbs or supplied by the LU. RUs consist of FM headers, program data (in the form of logical records), and protocol information.

Path control adds a "transmission header" (TH) to the BIU.

BIU Chains

A BIU chain consists of a sequence of BIUs transferred in one direction from one TP to another, without an intervening change of direction or confirmation. Thus, it corresponds exactly to a conversation message.

Bracket

A bracket consists of all chains transferred on a particular conversation. Thus, it corresponds exactly to the conversation itself. (See Figure 4-8.)

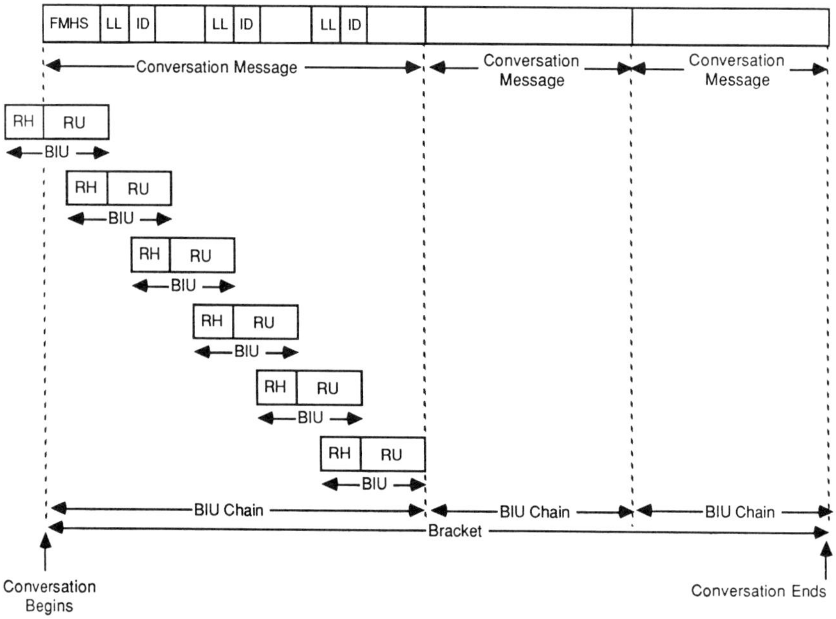

FMH = Function Management Header
LL = Logical Length
ID = Identifier
RU = Request/Response Unit
RH = RU Header
BIU = Basic Information Unit

Figure 4-8: Conversation Components

Chapter 5 - SNA Service Transaction Programs

5.1 Mapping LU6.2 Verbs to Service TP Commands

SNA defines a number of "service transaction programs." Service TPs offer services to application TPs. The application TPs use a command interface provided by the service TP. The service TP "maps" (translates) the basic LU verbs into a set of commands used by application TPs. The translation may simplify LU functions, or it may elaborate on them.

The service TPs use the LU6.2 protocol boundary in a manner prescribed by the LU6.2 architecture. For example, the architecture may limit which APPC verbs the service TP can use, and may specify values for parameters and variables. The architecture also specifies the "transaction program names" (TPNs) to be used for the service TPs.

Figure 5-1 shows how this process works with a particular service TP, namely, Document Interchange Architecture (DIA). The user program on the left issues a DIA command to the DIA service TP. The DIA service TP translates that command into LU6.2 verbs. Part of the data which the LU transfers is DIA protocol and command information. Another part of the data is user application data. The DIA service TP in this case provides the user program with a set of commands appropriate to document interchange, rather than the generalized set of LU6.2 commands, which are not designed particularly for document interchange.

Figure 5-2 shows how DIA translates a user's "sign-on" command into LU6.2 verbs.

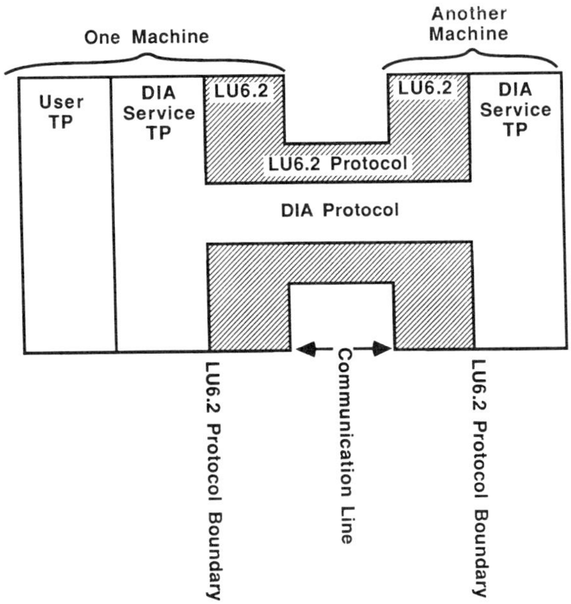

Figure 5-1: DIA Service TP

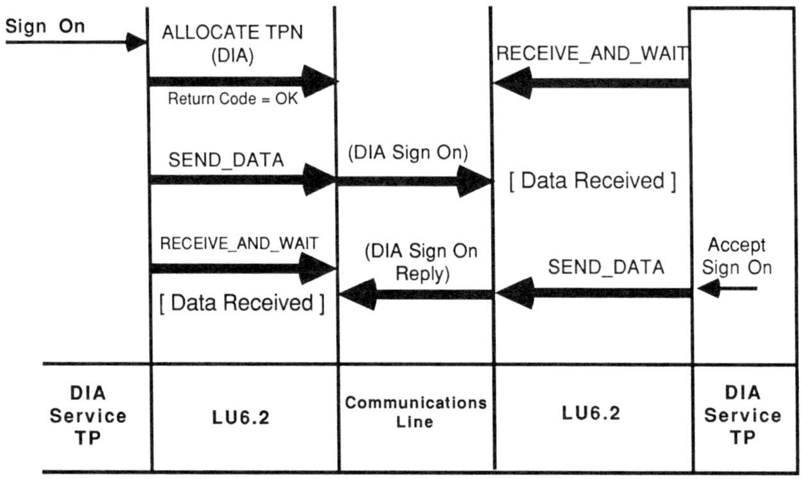

Figure 5-2: DIA and Command Translations

5.2 Characteristics of Service TPs

Service TPs differ from application TPs in a number of ways:

1) Service TPs use basic conversations at the LU6.2 protocol boundary. Application TPs usually use mapped conversations, but may use basic conversations, at the LU6.2 protocol boundary.

2) The names of service TPs are defined by SNA. The names of application TPs are arbitrarily defined by the user.

3) The command interface offered by service TPs is defined by SNA. Any command interface offered by an application TP would be defined by the application TP.

4) Service TPs are considered to be part of the LU. Application TPs are considered to be exterior to the LU.

5.3 The Control Operator TP

All LUs have at least one service TP, called the "control operator transaction program." This implementation-specific or installation-specific program is the control operator's interface with the LU. It performs the first three functions described for control verbs in section 4.7, namely: 1) create and modify data structures that define the LU and the network resources it can access (control points, transaction programs, partner LUs, and modes), 2) activate and deactivate sessions, 3) control numbers of sessions and "contention winner/contention loser" polarities of sessions.

5.4 The Change Number of Sessions (CNOS) TP

The fourth function mentioned in section 4.7, setting a limit on the number of parallel sessions permitted, involves a separate service TP, the "change number of sessions" (CNOS) service TP. When the control operator (at the source LU) invokes a CNOS function, the control operator TP issues a CNOS verb, which (after passing through the normal intermediate components, starting with presentation services) is received by the CNOS service TP (at the target LU) in the form of a GDS variable called a "CNOS command." The CNOS service TP and the control operator TP then negotiate the number of sessions allowed. (See Figure 5-3.)

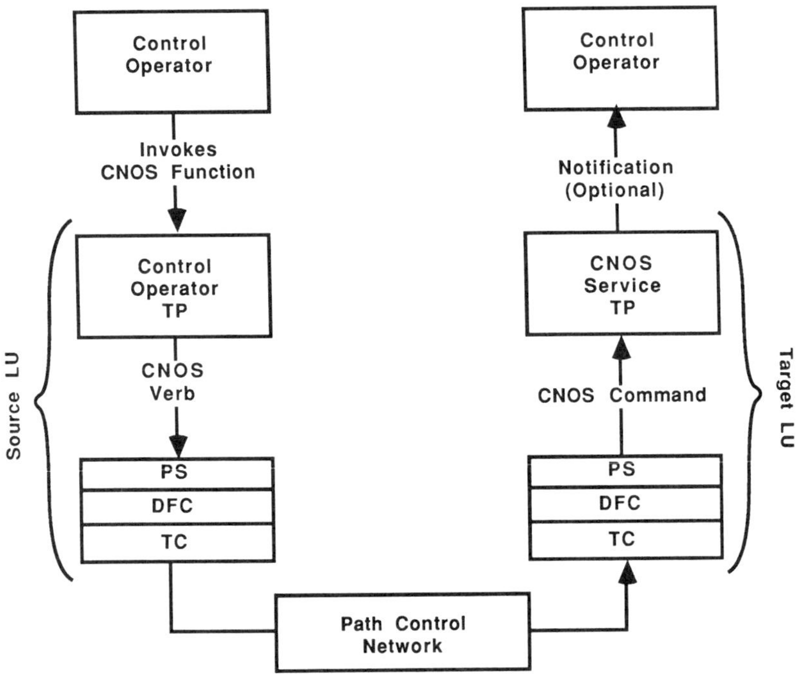

Components involved in executing the "change number of sessions" (CNOS) verb.

PS = Presentation Services
DFC = Data Flow Control
TC = Transmission Control

Figure 5-3: CNOS Service TP

5.5 Resynchronization

The resynchronization function of the sync point option is handled by the "sync point resynchronization transaction program." If an LU fails while executing the sync point protocol, one of the other LUs executing the sync point protocol starts the "resync" program at the failed LU as soon as the failed LU reinitializes. The failed LU starts the "resync" program at all its partner LUs. The resync TPs exchange information to determine whether their records are consistent concerning the transaction which they were processing when the LU failed. If not, they "back out" of the transaction.

5.6 SNA Distribution Services (SNADS)

SNA Distribution Services (SNADS) is an architecture which allows users on an SNA network to exchange many types of data. It is not limited to documents. The exchange is "asynchronous": the two end-points of the exchange do not need to be active on the network at the same time. SNADS is a "store-and-forward" service which will store information indefinitely and forward it to the next SNADS node on the path when the required communication line is active and available.

Application TPs or other service TPs issue verbs to SNADS to request distribution of data. A SNADS "distribution service unit" (DSU) responds to the request. A DSU is basically a collection of service TPs which provide such services as routing, storage, and distribution. Multiple DSUs, connected by sessions and conversations, form a SNADS network. (See Figure 5-4.)

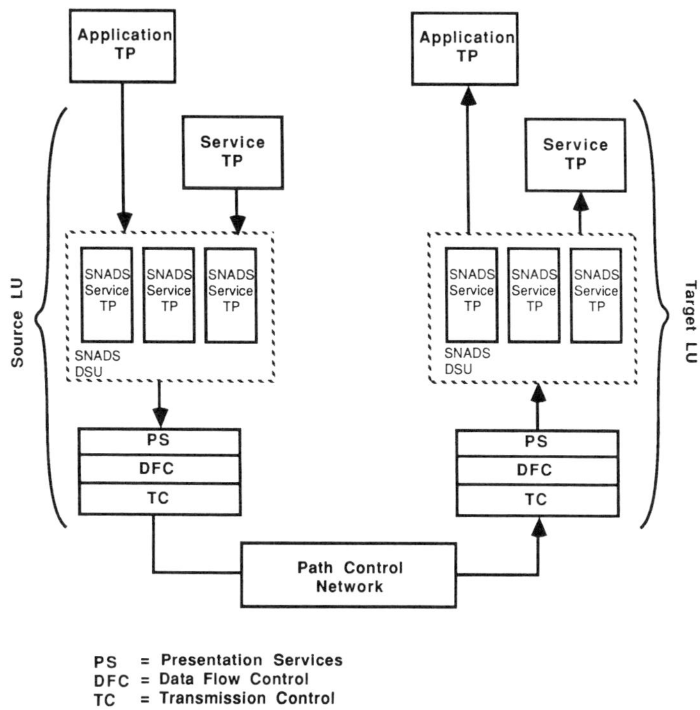

Figure 5-4: SNADS Components

5.7 Document Interchange Architecture (DIA)

Document Interchange Architecture (DIA) is a more limited architecture for data distribution. It also provides library services, allowing users to search a library of documents according to search criteria, and to retrieve documents from the library.

DIA is used by Source/Recipient Nodes (SRNs) attached to a single Office System Node (OSN). SRNs might be PCs running IBM's Personal Services/PC. An OSN might be a mainframe running DISOSS (Distributed Office Support System). DIA is designed to exchange only documents and messages, not other types of data.

DIA provides "synchronous" information transfer, in that both parties to the transfer must be active at the same time. However, the two parties to a DIA transfer are the SRN and the OSN. Thus, to transfer a message between two PCs, the first PC sends the message to the mainframe, where it can sit for any length of time. The second PC picks the message up at its convenience. The mainframe acts as a "mailbox." (See Figure 5-5.)

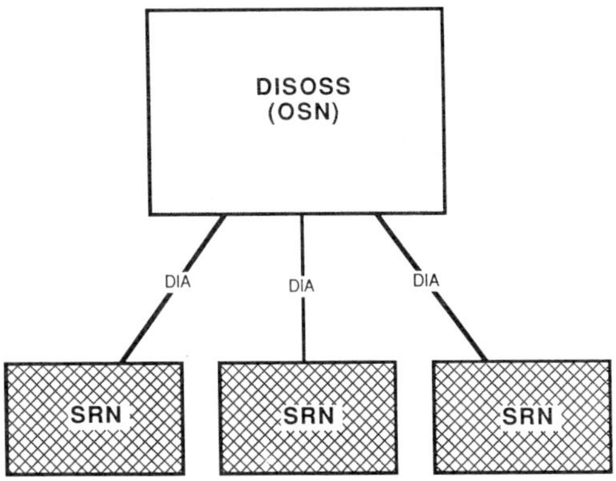

DISOSS = Distributed Office Support System
OSN = Office System Node
DIA = Document Interchange Architecture
SRN = Source/Recipient Node

Figure 5-5: DIA Components

DIA is implemented as a set of service TPs. Normally, each instance of DIA is one service TP using one conversation.

5.8 How SNADS and DIA Work Together

A single mainframe may be both a DIA OSN and a SNADS DSU. Suppose two such mainframes are connected in an SNA network. If a DIA message or document originates at an SRN attached to one mainframe, but is destined for an SRN attached to the other mainframe, the information is passed from one mainframe to the other using SNADS. (See Figure 5-6.)

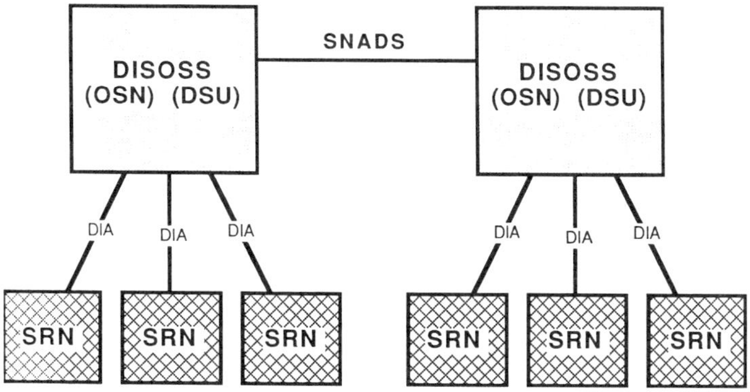

DISOSS = Distributed Office Support System
OSN = Office System Node
DSU = Distribution Service Unit
DIA = Document Interchange Architecture
SRN = Source/Recipient Node

Figure 5-6: SNADS, DIA Interoperability

DISOSS handles the OSN side of the DIA transfer. It also serves as an intermediary between DIA and SNADS. When a user issues a DIA "sign-on request," the user is actually asking to begin a session with DISOSS. A DIA distribution request is actually a request to DISOSS to perform the distribution. Once the request is made, the document resides in a DISOSS queue, and the DIA user logs off. It is now up to DISOSS to distribute the document. If the recipient is an SRN on the same OSN as the sender, DISOSS leaves the document in the output queue. The recipient then logs on, requests a list of documents in the output queue, and retrieves the document through another DIA session.

If, on the other hand, the user is on a different mainframe, DISOSS recognizes this fact and sends the document to that other mainframe using SNADS. If communication facilities are not immediately available, DISOSS queues the document for later transmission.

Thus, there are two different types of data exchange: One between an SRN and an OSN (DIA), and another between two DSUs (SNADS). The SNADS transfer is always based on LU6.2. The DIA transfer is typically based on LU6.2.

5.9 Distributed Data Management (DDM)

The Distributed Data Management (DDM) architecture discussed in sections 1.8 and 3.4 is supported by a "distributed data management synchronous conversation transaction program" in each DDM node.

5.10 Other Service TPs

Some SNA service TPs are product-specific. For example, there is a "virtual disk transaction program" and a "virtual printer transaction program" for the IBM System/36 and the IBM System/38.

There are also service TPs developed under LU6.1 which will run under LU6.2. For example, LU6.1 features a "scheduler TP" and a "queue TP."

Sample APPC Verb Usage

6.1 Overview

This chapter contains several short, simple examples of how APPC verbs are used. These are not actual programs, but a type of "pseudocode" which outlines some of the basic actions which might be performed by actual programs. The examples use basic conversation verbs, but the principles illustrated apply to mapped conversation verbs, too.

In each example, two transaction programs are connected by a conversation. The programs are referred to as TP "a" and TP "b."

Information transferred from one TP to the other is shown as an arrow (--->).

A vertical line under a verb (|) indicates that the LU suspends the TP's processing until the LU completes the verb.

Significant parameters are shown with the verbs. For example, the TYPE parameter with the supplied value of LOCAL is shown as TYPE(LOCAL). The RETURN_CODE parameter with the returned value OK is shown as RETURN_CODE=OK. Non-significant parameters are omitted.

Notes accompany each example. The notes are numbered; the numbers correspond with the numbers in parentheses in the example.

Comments within the example are bracketed: [end conversation].

Section 4.5 contains a similar example.

1. TP "a" issues ALLOCATE verb, requesting a conversation with TP "b."

2. TP "a" requests confirmation processing. If TP "b" accepts the ALLOCATE, either LU will be able to request confirmation of certain transmissions.

3. LU "a" places the allocation request in the send buffer. (The allocation request is also called a "function management header 5" or FMH 5.) The conversation is now in send state from the point of view of TP "a." Nothing is sent.

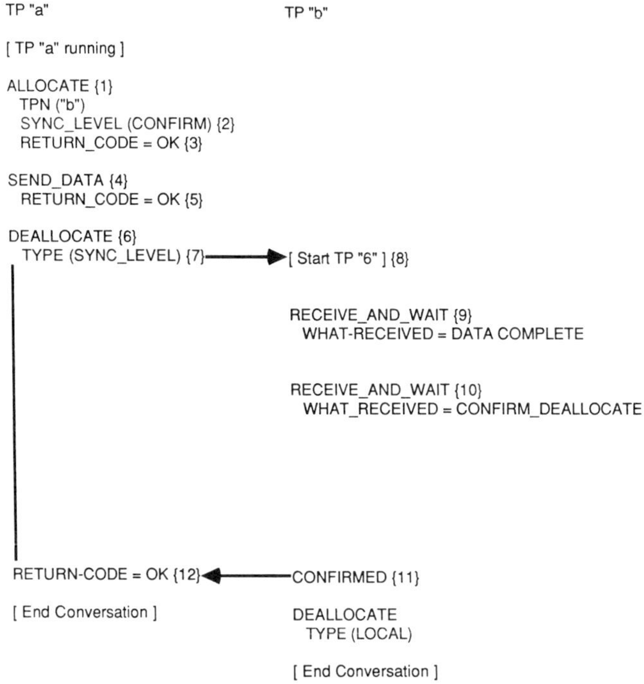

Figure 6-1: ALLOCATE, SEND, DEALLOCATE With CONFIRM

4. TP "a" issues the SEND_DATA verb.

5. The LU successfully places the data in the send buffer. Nothing is sent. (Since this is a basic conversation, the data could be any number of complete or partial logical records. However, for the sake of simplicity, the example assumes that the TP places exactly one logical record in the buffer. If this were a mapped conversation, the data would have to consist of exactly one data record.)

6. TP "a" issues the DEALLOCATE verb. This places a CONFIRM_ DEALLOCATE in the send buffer. The entire contents of the buffer are then sent.

7. TYPE(SYNC_LEVEL) means that the synchronization level of the DEALLOCATE is the same as the synchronization level of the ALLOCATE, namely, CONFIRM. This means that TP "b" will have to perform confirmation processing, and that TP "a" will suspend processing until it receives a confirmation (positive or negative) from TP "b."

8. TP "b" is started. This is done in an implementation-specific or installation-specific manner. For example, in APPC/PC, the application subsystem would start

TP "b" using the GET_ALLOCATE verb. No LU-defined verbs are used.

9. TP "b" receives the data with one RECEIVE_AND_WAIT verb issuance. The WHAT_RECEIVED=DATA_COMPLETE results from the fact that the FILL parameter on the RECEIVE_AND_WAIT verb was set to LL, meaning that TP "b" elects to receive just one logical record at a time. (The allocation request, also called a "function management header 5" or FMH 5, is stripped off by LU "b" and does not reach TP "b.")

10. TP "b" receives the CONFIRM_DEALLOCATE with a second RECEIVE_AND_WAIT verb issuance. (Note: Some implementations may not require a second RECEIVE_AND_WAIT, but will receive the data and the CONFIRM_DEALLOCATE with one RECEIVE_AND_WAIT.)

11. TP "b" gives LU "a" permission to deallocate the conversation by issuing the CONFIRMED verb. Alternatively, by issuing the SEND_ERROR verb, TP "b" could have told LU "a" not to deallocate the conversation.

12. When TP "a" receives the confirmation (in the form of an OK return code), the DEALLOCATE verb completes, and the conversation ends from the point of view of TP "a."

13. TP "b" issues a local DEALLOCATE. LU "b" discards its control information for the conversation. The conversation ends from the point of view of TP "b."

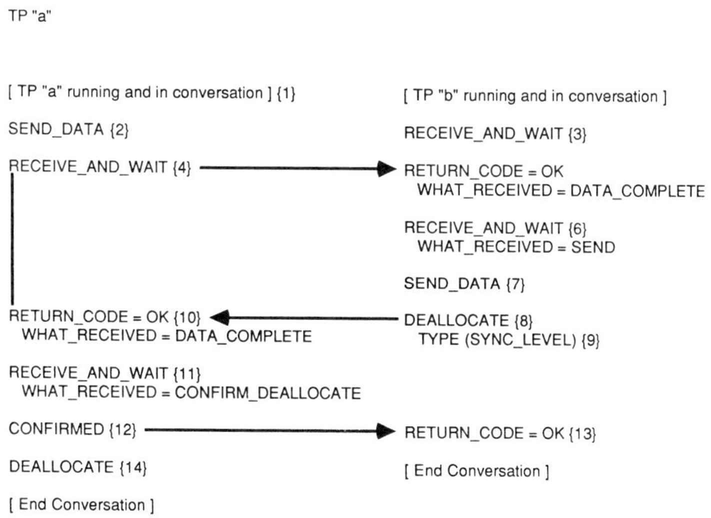

Figure 6-2: SEND, "FLIP FLOP" And RECEIVE, DEALLOCATE, With Confirm

1. TP "a" has allocated a conversation with TP "b." The sync level is CONFIRM. The conversation is in send state for TP "a" and receive state for TP "b."

2. TP "a" issues the SEND_DATA verb. LU "a" places the data in the send buffer. Nothing is sent. (Since this is a basic conversation, the data could be any number of complete or partial logical records. However, for the sake of simplicity, the example assumes that TP "a" sends exactly one logical record.)

3. TP "b" issues the RECEIVE_AND_WAIT verb. Since the conversation is in receive state on the "b" side, this verb does not generate a flow over the communication line. (Contrast this with step 4.) Since no information has arrived, the verb does not complete. LU "b" suspends TP "b" processing until the verb completes.

4. TP "a" issues RECEIVE_AND_WAIT. Since the conversation is in send state on the "a" side, this causes LU "a" to "flip-flop" the conversation. This entails placing a SEND indication in the send buffer, sending the entire contents of the buffer, and putting the conversation into receive state on the "a" side. LU "a" then suspends TP "a" processing until the RECEIVE_AND_WAIT verb completes. (The technical term for the SEND indication is the "change direction indicator" or CDI.)

5. LU "b" revives TP "b" because the RECEIVE_AND_WAIT verb issued in step 3 above has completed, now that information has arrived. (Since this is a basic conversation, the data received could be any number of complete or partial logical records. This example assumes that, by setting the FILL parameter to LL, TP "b" has elected to receive just one logical record at a time.)

6. TP "b" receives the SEND indication by issuing another RECEIVE_AND_WAIT. (Some implementations of the architecture may receive the data and the SEND indication with one RECEIVE_AND_WAIT.)

7. TP "b" issues a SEND_DATA verb, causing the LU "b" to place data in the send buffer. Nothing is sent. (Since this is a basic conversation, the data could be any number of complete or partial logical records.)

8. TP "b" issues a DEALLOCATE. The LU places a CONFIRM_DEALLOCATE in the send buffer, sends the entire contents of the buffer, and suspends TP "b" processing, awaiting a response, positive or negative.

9. TYPE(SYNC_LEVEL) means that the DEALLOCATE has the same sync level as the ALLOCATE. In the example, the sync level is assumed to be CONFIRM. (Had the sync level been NONE, the LU would have placed a DEALLOCATE in the send buffer and would not have suspended TP "b" processing.)

10. LU "a" receives information from TP "b." The RECEIVE_AND_WAIT issued in step 4 above completes, and LU "a" revives TP "a." (Since this is a basic conversation, the data could be any number of complete or partial logical records. By setting the FILL parameter to LL, the TP can elect to receive just one logical record at a time.)

11. TP "a" receives the CONFIRM_DEALLOCATE by issuing another RECEIVE_AND_WAIT.

12. TP "a" issues a CONFIRMED, indicating that it consents to the deallocation.

13. LU "b" receives the confirmation. LU "b" ends the conversation (discards control information) on the "b" side and returns control to TP "b."

14. TP "a" issues a local DEALLOCATE. LU "a" discards control information pertaining to the conversation. The conversation ends on the "a" side.

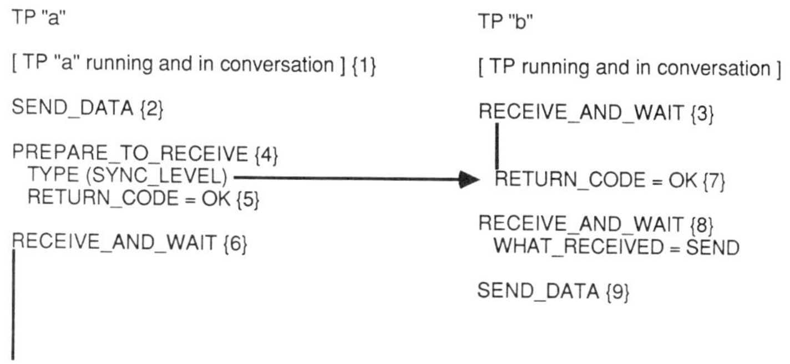

Figure 6-3: SEND, PREPARE TO RECEIVE, And RECEIVE

1. The conversation is in send state for TP "a" and receive state for TP "b." TP "a" has allocated the conversation with SYNC_LEVEL(NONE).

2. TP "a" issues the SEND_DATA verb. The LU places the data in its send buffer. Nothing is sent.

3. TP "b" issues the RECEIVE_AND_WAIT verb. LU "b" suspends TP "b" processing, awaiting the arrival of information.

4. TP "a" issues the PREPARE_TO_RECEIVE verb. TYPE(SYNC_LEVEL) means synchronization matches that of the conversation. In this example, the conversation was allocated with SYNC_LEVEL(NONE). LU "a" places a SEND indication in the send buffer, sends the entire contents of the buffer, and puts the conversation in receive state on the "a" side. (The technical term for the SEND indication is the "change direction indicator" or CDI.)

5. The PREPARE_TO_RECEIVE completes immediately. No confirmation is required because the synchronization level is NONE. (Alternatively, with sync level CONFIRM, TP "a" would suspend until the confirmation was received.)

6. TP "a" issues RECEIVE_AND_WAIT. LU "a" suspends TP "a" processing, awaiting arriving information.

7. LU "b" receives the data from TP "a." The RECEIVE_AND_WAIT issued in step 3 above completes.

8. TP "b" issues a second RECEIVE_AND_WAIT and receives the SEND indication.

9. Since TP "b" has received the SEND indication, the conversation is in send state on the "b" side. TP "b" issues the SEND_DATA verb.

Appendix A: The APPC Verbs

MAPPED CONVERSATION VERBS

MC_ALLOCATE
MC_CONFIRM
MC_CONFIRMED
MC_DEALLOCATE
MC_FLUSH
MC_GET_ATTRIBUTES
MC_POST_ON_RECEIPT
MC_PREPARE_TO_RECEIVE
MC_RECEIVE_AND_WAIT
MC_RECEIVE_IMMEDIATE
MC_REQUEST_TO_SEND
MC_SEND_DATA
MC_SEND_ERROR
MC_TEST

TYPE-INDEPENDENT CONVERSATION VERBS

BACKOUT
GET_TYPE
SYNCPT
WAIT

BASIC CONVERSATION VERBS

ALLOCATE
CONFIRM
CONFIRMED
DEALLOCATE
FLUSH
GET_ATTRIBUTES
POST_ON_RECEIPT
PREPARE_TO_RECEIVE
RECEIVE_AND_WAIT
RECEIVE_IMMEDIATE
REQUEST_TO_SEND
SEND_DATA
SEND_ERROR
TEST

CONTROL-OPERATOR VERBS

Change Number of Sessions Verbs

CHANGE_SESSION_LIMIT
INITIALIZE_SESSION_LIMIT
RESET_SESSION_LIMIT
PROCESS_SESSION_LIMIT

Session Control Verbs

ACTIVATE_SESSION
DEACTIVATE_SESSION

LU Definition Verbs

DEFINE_LOCAL_LU
DEFINE_REMOTE_LU
DEFINE_MODE
DEFINE_TP
DISPLAY_LOCAL_LU
DISPLAY_REMOTE_LU
DISPLAY_MODE
DISPLAY_TP
DELETE

Appendix B: APPC/PC Implementation of the LU6.2 Architecture

This appendix lists the option subsets supported by the APPC/PC implementation of LU6.2. It also shows how APPC/PC verbs correspond to verbs defined by the architecture.

Supported Option Subsets

Immediate allocation of a session

Allows a program to allocate a "contention-winner" session if one is available immediately. If a contention-winner session is not available, the attempt to allocate a session fails. (When two programs attempt to allocate a conversation on the same session at the same time, the "contention winner" gets to allocate the conversation. See section 2.6, 4.6, and 5.3.)

Session level LU-LU verification

Permits a program or operator to provide passwords to be used by remote LUs to verify their identify when a session is activated.

User ID verification

Verifies that incoming allocate requests should be accepted from a particular user ID.

Program-supplied user ID and password

Allows the program allocating a conversation to specify the user ID and password to be sent on the allocation request.

Program Initialization Parameters (PIP) data (send only)

Permits the program allocating a conversation to supply "program initialization parameters" (PIPs) with the allocation request. PIPs are defined and supplied by the application TP. They are not interpreted by the LU.

Logging of data in a system log

Allows the program to record error data in the system error log.

Flush the LU's send buffer

Permits the program to force the LU to send everything in its send buffer. (Note that "flush" here does not imply discarding the information, as it does in some contexts.)

Prepare to receive

Allows the program to issue the "prepare to receive" verb which flushes the LU's send buffer and changes the state of the conversation from send to receive. The program can also request confirmation.

Long Locks

This is an option of the "prepare to receive" verb. Permits the remote LU to send confirmation and data in one operation, rather than separately.

Post on receipt with wait

APPC/PC implements this only for basic conversations, as the "post on receipt" and "wait" verbs. Allows a program to request posting to a particular conversation when data arrives for that conversation, and then to wait until the data arrives.

Post on receipt with test for posting

APPC/PC implements this only for basic conversations, as the "post on receipt" and "test" verb. Permits a program to request posting to a particular conversation, and then tests to see whether information is available. (There is a mapped conversation "test" verb, but it does not test for posting. See "test for request-to-send received" below.)

Receive immediate

Allows the program to receive any information that is available for the conversation, but does not wait for information to arrive. Does not require posting.

Test for request-to-send received

Permits a program to test whether a "request to send" notification has been received.

Get attributes

Allows a program to get the "attributes" of a mapped conversation. Attributes include the LU ID, the network name, the network name of the LU, the name of the partner LU, the name of the partner's LU, the mode name, the sync level, and the user ID if the program specified conversation-level security.

Get conversation type

Permits a program to determine whether it should use mapped or basic verbs with a particular conversation.

Mapped conversation LU services component

This option is available in all "open API" implementations of the LU, that is, all implementations which support arbitrary user-written programs. (See section 4.8) Allows implementation of an "mapped conversation LU services component" program, which processes mapped conversation verbs. This option enables the program to use mapped verbs. It is different from the "data mapping" option (which APPC/PC does not offer) which allows the program to request mapping of data by local and remote LUs.

MIN_COWINNERS_TARGET parameter

A parameter of the "change number of sessions" (CNOS) verb. Permits a program or operator at the LU issuing the verb to request that the minimum number of contention winner sessions at the target LU be greater than zero.

RESPONSIBLE(TARGET) parameter

A parameter of the "change number of sessions" (CNOS) verb. Allows a program or operator at the LU issuing the verb to request that the target LU be responsible for session deactivations when the verb requires that the number of active sessions be decreased.

DRAIN_TARGET(NO) parameter

A parameter of the "change number of sessions" (CNOS) verb. Permits a program or operator at the LU issuing the verb (the source LU) to request that the target LU be unable to "drain" the target LU's allocation requests by resetting the (LU,mode) session limit to zero. "Draining" occurs when the LU continues to allocate conversation requests to sessions until no conversation requests remain, after which time the LU rejects requests.

LU-parameter verbs

Allows a program or operator to specify the operating parameters of its own LU. The parameters are product-dependent. This option is implemented as the "attach LU" verb in APPC/PC. Parameters include the LU name, the LU local address, and the LU session limit.

LU-LU session limit

Permits a program or operator to limit the number of LU-LU sessions. Implemented with the "attach LU" verb as the "LU session limit" and "partner LU session limit" supplied parameters.

Maximum RU size bounds

Allows a program or operator to set the bounds (lower and upper) for maximum RU size on sessions in an (LU,mode) group.

Contention winner automatic activation limit

Permits a program or operator to set a limit on the number of sessions which can be automatically activated as contention-winners within an (LU, mode) group. The "change number of sessions" (CNOS) verb has an "auto activate" parameter which specifies contention-winner sessions to be activated automatically by APPC/PC, rather than by allocation requests from transaction programs.

LU6.2 VERBS AND APPC/PC VERBS

BASIC CONVERSATION VERBS

LU6.2 Architecture

ALLOCATE
BACKOUT
CONFIRM
CONFIRMED
DEALLOCATE
FLUSH
GET_ATTRIBUTES
GET_TYPE
POST_ON_RECEIPT
PREPARE_TO_RECEIVE
RECEIVE_AND_WAIT
RECEIVE_IMMEDIATE
REQUEST_TO_SEND
SEND_DATA
SEND_ERROR
SYNCPT
TEST
WAIT

APPC/PC Implementation

ALLOCATE

CONFIRM
CONFIRMED
DEALLOCATE
FLUSH
GET_ATTRIBUTES
GET_TYPE
POST_ON_RECEIPT
PREPARE_TO_RECEIVE
RECEIVE_AND_WAIT
RECEIVE_IMMEDIATE
REQUEST_TO_SEND
SEND_DATA
SEND_ERROR

TEST
WAIT

Note: BACKOUT and SYNCPT are not supported, because APPC/PC does not support the sync point option.

LU6.2 VERBS AND APPC/PC VERBS

MAPPED CONVERSATION VERBS

LU6.2 Architecture

BACKOUT
GET_TYPE
MC_ALLOCATE
MC_CONFIRM
MC_CONFIRMED
MC_DEALLOCATE
MC_FLUSH
MC_GET_ATTRIBUTES
MC_POST_ON_RECEIPT
MC_PREPARE_TO_RECEIVE
MC_RECEIVE_AND_WAIT
MC_RECEIVE_IMMEDIATE
MC_REQUEST_TO_SEND
MC_SEND_DATA
MC_SEND_ERROR
MC_TEST
SYNCPT
WAIT

APPC/PC Implementation

GET_TYPE
MC_ALLOCATE
MC_CONFIRM
MC_CONFIRMED
MC_DEALLOCATE
MC_FLUSH
MC_GET_ATTRIBUTES

MC_PREPARE_TO_RECEIVE
MC_RECEIVE_AND_WAIT
MC_RECEIVE_IMMEDIATE
MC_REQUEST_TO_SEND

MC_SEND_DATA
MC_SEND_ERROR
MC_TEST

Note: BACKOUT and SYNCPT are not supported, because APPC/PC does not support the sync point option.

Note: WAIT is an option of POST_AND_RECEIVE.

LU6.2 VERBS AND APPC/PC VERBS

OTHER VERBS

LU6.2 Architecture

APPC/PC Implementation

TRANSFER_MS_DATA

CONVERT

PASSTHROUGH

SET_PASSTHROUGH

TRACE

Note: TRANSFER_MS_DATA is referred to as the "network management verb." It allows a transaction program to send management services information to a system services control point (SSCP) which manages the network with the help of this information. Information includes alerts, problem determination statistics (PDSTATS), and other network management data.

Appendix C: Acronyms And Abbreviations

API	-	application programming interface
APPC	-	Advanced Program-to-Program Communication
APPC/PC	-	APPC for the Personal Computer
APPN	-	Application-to-Application Networking
BIU	-	basic information unit
CDI	-	change direction indicator
CICS	-	Customer Information Control System
CNOS	-	change number of sessions
CPU	-	central processing unit
DCA	-	Document Content Architecture
DDM	-	Distributed Data Management
DFC	-	data flow control
DIA	-	Document Interchange Architecture
DISOSS	-	Distributed Office Support System
DLC	-	data link control
DPPX	-	Distributed Processing Program Executive
DSS	-	Distributed Systems Services
DSU	-	distribution service unit
EDD	-	electronic document distribution
FMH	-	function management header
GDS	-	general data stream
HS	-	half-session
ID	-	identifier (prefix)
ISC	-	Intelligent Serial Controller
ISO	-	International Organization for Standardization
LL	-	logical record length (prefix)
LLID	-	logical record length and GDS ID (prefix)
LNS	-	LU network services
LU	-	logical unit
MC	-	mapped conversation
MCR	-	MC record
MU	-	message unit
NAU	-	network addressable unit
NCP	-	Network Control Program
OSI	-	Open Systems Interconnection
OSN	-	Office System Node
PC	-	path control
PIP	-	program initialization parameter
PS	-	presentation services

PU - physical unit
RH - request/response header
RISC - Reduced Instruction Set Computer
RM - resources manager
RT - RISC Technology
PC-RT - Personal Computer-RT
RU - request/response unit
SDLC - Synchronous Data Link Control
SNA - Systems Network Architecture
SNADS - SNA Distribution Services
SRN - Source/Recipient Node
SSCP - system services control point
TC - transmission control
TH - transmission header
TP - transaction program

Appendix D: References

1. Czubek, Don, "APPN an evolving solution," *Network World*, June 30, 1986, p. 17.

2. Digital Equipment Corporation, *Digital's Solution to Multivendor Networking*, 1986.

3. IBM Corporation, *Advanced Program-to-Program Communication for the Personal Computer, Programming Guide, SC30-3396.*

4. IBM Corporation, *APPC/PC Installation and Configuration Guide, GC30-3397.*

5. IBM Corporation, *An Introduction to Advanced Program-to-Program Communication (APPC), GG24-1584.*

6. IBM Corporation, *CICS/VS Version 1 Release 6 Application Programmer's Reference Manual Command Level, SC33-0077.*

7. IBM Corporation, *CICS/VS Version 1 Release 6 Intercommunication Facilities Guide, SC33-0133.*

8. IBM Corporation, *Document Interchange Architecture: Final-Form-Text Reference, SC23-0757.*

9. IBM Corporation, *Document Interchange Architecture: Revisable-Form-Text Reference, SC23-0758.*

10. IBM Corporation, *Document Interchange Architecture: Concepts and Structures, SC23-0759.*

11. IBM Corporation, *Document Interchange Architecture: Document Library Services Reference, SC23-0760.*

12. IBM Corporation, *Document Interchange Architecture: Application Processing Services Reference, SC23-0761.*

13. IBM Corporation, *Document Interchange Architecture: Document Distribution Services Reference, SC23-0762.*

14. IBM Corporation, *Document Interchange Architecture: Transaction Programmer's Guide, SC23-0763.*

15. IBM Corporation, *Document Interchange Architecture: Interchange Document Profile Reference, SC23-0764.*

16. IBM Corporation, *IBM SDLC General Information, GA27-3093.*

17. IBM Corporation, *Office Information Architectures: Concepts, GC23-0765.*

18. IBM Corporation, *Systems and Products Guide, Tenth Edition, G320-6300- 09,* July 1986.

19. IBM Corporation, *Systems Network Architecture APPC in a Peer CICS/VS Environment, GG24-1656.*

20. IBM Corporation, *Systems Network Architecture - Concepts and Products, GC30-3072.*

21. IBM Corporation, *Systems Network Architecture Format and Protocol Reference Manual, SC30-3112.*

22. IBM Corporation, *Systems Network Architecture Format and Protocol Reference Manual: Architecture for LU Type 6.2, SC30-3269.*

23. IBM Corporation, *Systems Network Architecture Reference Summary, GA27-3136.*

24. IBM Corporation, *Systems Network Architecture Introduction, GA27-3116.*

25. IBM Corporation, *Systems Network Architecture - General Information, GA27-3102.*

26. IBM Corporation, *Systems Network Architecture - Sessions Between Logical Units, GC20-1868.*

27. IBM Corporation, *System Network Architecture Transaction Programmer's Reference Manual for LU Type 6.2, GC30-3084.*

28. IBM Corporation, *Systems Network Architecture: Technical Overview, GC30-3073.*

Glossary

Advanced Program-to-Program Communication (APPC)

An architecture for peer-to-peer, application-to-application programming. Also called LU6.2.

Advanced Program-to-Program Communication for the Personal Computer (APPC/PC)

An implementation of APPC for the IBM Personal Computer family.

alert

The main network management message for forwarding problem determination information to a network operator.

allocate

To assign a resource, such as a conversation or session, to an entity which will use it, such as a transaction program or LU.

Applications Programming Interface (API)

A protocol boundary which can be used by arbitrary user-written programs.

application program

A program which accomplishes something directly for the end user.

application subsystem

In APPC/PC, a portion of the LU which is installation-specific, written by an end-user programmer. The application subsystem consists of one or more transaction programs which provice services to application transaction programs and to APPC/PC.

Application-to-Application Networking (APPN)

A capability based on enhancements to LU6.2 and PU2.1, which allows peripheral nodes to perform intermediate routing functions on an SNA network.

basic conversation

A conversation using basic conversation verbs. Typically used by service transaction programs.

basic conversation verb

A type of APPC verb which allows the programmer to send any number of partial or complete logical records. Contrast with mapped conversation verbs, which may be used when the implementation supports the "mapped conversation LU services component" option.

boundary function

Services, such as message re-formatting and address translation, which an intermediate or host node provides to a peripheral node in an SNA network.

CICS

A mainframe teleprocessing monitor, Customer Information Control System.

confirmation

Acknowledgement by a transaction program that data has been received and successfully processed. When the data includes a request, confirmation can be positive (request granted) or negative (request denied).

contention loser

When two LUs attempt to allocate conversations on the same session at the same time, the contention loser is the LU that cannot allocate a conversation on the session without permission from the partner LU.

contention-loser polarity

The condition of being a contention loser.

contention winner

When two LUs attempt to allocate conversations on the same session at the same time, the contention winner is the LU that cannot allocate a conversation on the session without permission from the partner LU.

control verb

An APPC verb used to manipulate certain aspects of the LU or the LU's environment, such as the PU. See section 4.7.

conversation

A logical connection between two transaction programs.

conversation type

There are two types of conversations: mapped and basic.

conversation verb

A verb used to communicate with a remote program.

Customer Information Control System for Virtual Storage (CICS/VS)

A "teleprocessing monitor" for host computers. Designed to reduce the effort required for terminal-oriented transaction programming by interfacing between user-written applications and the "teleprocessing access method" (e.g. VTAM) and database manager (e.g. SQL/DS or DB2).

distributed processing

Processing performed by cooperating machines which are geographically separated from one another, and connected by a communications network.

drain

Draining occurs when the LU continues to allocate conversation requests to sessions until no conversation requests remain, after which time the LU rejects requests.

flush

To force the LU to send the information in its send buffer. Information is not discarded.

function management header 5 (FMH 5)

An optional field at the beginning of a request unit (RU) which requests that the remote LU allocate a conversation for a particular transaction program.

Two other types of FMHs are used by LU6.2. FMH 7 describes an error. FMH 12 carries LU-LU password verification data.

General Data Stream (GDS)

A means of formatting information for transfer over an SNA network. The basic unit of the GDS is the GDS variable.

host node

A subarea node, such as a mainframe computer, containing a system services control point (SSCP).

Logical Unit (LU)

Code residing in a machine on a network, either in firmware or in software, which allows the machine to communicate on the network. The LU provides services to the end user, and may be thought of as the end user's "port" into the network.

mapped conversation

A conversation using mapped conversation verbs. Typically used by an end user transaction program to communicate with another end user transaction program. See sections 2.1 and 4.6.

mapped conversation verb

A verb used in a mapped conversation. Typically used by an end user transaction program to communicate with another end user transaction program. See sections 2.1 and 4.6.

mode

A set of implementation-specific or installation-specific parameters defining the properties of a session, such as the highest synchronization level allowed, the class of service for sessions, and routing and delay characteristics of sessions.

mode name

Name for a mode, used to classify sessions so that various operations can be performed on a subset of sessions. See, under "Supported Option Subsets" in Appendix B:

DRAIN_TARGET(NO) parameter
Maximum RU size bounds

Network Addressable Unit (NAU)

An addressable entity on an SNA network. There are three kinds of NAUs: LUs, PUs, and SSCPs.

network management verb

In APPC/PC, the verb TRANSFER_MS_DATA, used to send network management information to a network management services functions.

node

A machine at the end of a link, or at the intersection of two or more links on an SNA network. Terminals, communications controllers, and host processors are all nodes.

parallel sessions

Two or more sessions between the same two LUs.

partner transaction programs

Two transaction programs communicating over a single conversation.

path control network

The part of the SNA network to which the LU hands information for routing to another LU.

peer-to-peer communication

Communication between two LUs without an intermediate host.

peripheral node

A node on an SNA network that does not perform intermediate network routing functions.

Physical Unit (PU)

A component of an SNA node that manages network resources, such as communication lines.

program initialization parameters (PIPs)

Information which may optionally be exchanged by transaction programs when a conversation is allocated. PIPs are defined by the application programmer.

posting

Running a particular section of code when an event occurs. In APPC, this technique may optionally be used when information arrives, using the POST_ON_RECEIPT verb.

request/response header (RH)

A prefix field in an RU (request/response unit), containing control information pertaining to the RU.

responsible LU

The LU designated to deactivate a session. Used in connection with the "change number of sessions" (CNOS) verb, which may require that the number of active sessions be decreased. See, under "Supported Option Subsets" in Appendix B:

RESPONSIBLE(TARGET) parameter

session

A logical connection between two NAUs.

state

The four states of a conversation are reset, send, receive, and confirm. The state determines what verbs a transaction program can issue on a conversation. See section ??

subset

A group of optional APPC capabilities which must be implemented together, if at all.

synchronization level

The three synchronization levels (none, confirm, sync point) determine whether and how two transaction programs confirm and coordinate sending and receiving of data.

Synchronous Data Link Control (SDLC)

A low-level communications protocol which can support APPC.

Systems Network Architecture (SNA)

IBM's master plan for allowing its products to communicate, SNA defines logical structures, formats, protocols, and procedures for exchanging information on a data communications network.

system services control point (SSCP)

A control point in a host node which performs services for dependent nodes, such as bringing up the network, establishing sessions, or recovering when a component fails to maintain contact.

transaction

A logical unit of work, from the point of view of an application program on a network.

transaction program

An application program which performs transactions in cooperation with one or more other application programs on a network.

Virtual Telecommunications Access Method (VTAM)

A group of programs supporting terminal-to-host communications. APPC works at a higher level than VTAM in a host node.

Index

About The Author...

Michael Hurwicz is an independent local area network specialist based in Nashville, Tennessee. His articles appear regularly in a variety of trade publications. His work with LAN technology includes analysis, decision support, design, and implementation, as well as technical documentation, editing, and translating. Mr. Hurwicz received a Masters Degree in French from the University of Minnesota, and an Associate of Arts degree in Electronics Technology from Brown Institute in Minneapolis.

Other Books of Interest from Architecture Technology Corporation

Inside The Token-Ring -- J. Scott Haugdahl
Inside NETBIOS -- J. Scott Haugdahl